THE CRY FOR HELP
and the Professional Response

by

JACK KAHN, M.D., F.R.C.Psych., D.P.M.
formerly Community Psychiatrist,
London Borough of Newham, and
Consultant Child Psychiatrist, Whittington Hospital

and

ELSPETH EARLE, M.B., B.S., M.R.C.Psych.,
Consultant in Adult Mental Illness at Queen Charlotte's
Maternity Hospital, Child Psychiatrist at
The Middlesex Hospital, and Practising Psychoanalyst

PERGAMON PRESS
OXFORD · NEW YORK · TORONTO · SYDNEY · PARIS · FRANKFURT

U.K.	Pergamon Press Ltd., Headington Hill Hall, Oxford OX3 0BW, England
U.S.A.	Pergamon Press Inc., Maxwell House, Fairview Park, Elmsford, New York 10523, U.S.A.
CANADA	Pergamon Press Canada Ltd., Suite 104, 150 Consumers Road, Willowdale, Ontario M2J 1P9, Canada
AUSTRALIA	Pergamon Press (Aust.) Pty. Ltd., P.O. Box 544, Potts Point, N.S.W. 2011, Australia
FRANCE	Pergamon Press SARL, 24 rue des Ecoles, 75240 Paris, Cedex 05, France
FEDERAL REPUBLIC OF GERMANY	Pergamon Press GmbH, 6242 Kronberg-Taunus, Hammerweg 6, Federal Republic of Germany

First edition 1982

Library of Congress Cataloging in Publication Data

Kahn, Jack H.
The cry for help—and the professional response.
(Social work series) (Pergamon international library of science, technology, engineering, and social studies)
1. Social service. I. Earle, Elspeth. II. Title. III. Series: Pergamon international library of science, technology, engineering, and social studies.
HV31.K325   1982   361.3   81-21110   AACR2

British Library Cataloguing in Publication Data

Kahn, Jack
The cry for help: and the professional response.—
(Social work series)
1. Psychiatry
I. Title II. Earle, Elspeth III. Series
616.89'002436   RC454

ISBN 0-08-027438-2 hardcover
ISBN 0-08-027437-4 flexicover

Printed in Great Britain by A. Wheaton & Co. Ltd., Exeter

A Personal Note

AT THE end of the task of writing this book it was possible to look back at the beginning, and Elspeth Earle suggested that I should recall some of the original thoughts in a personal note.

I had been preoccupied for some years with two themes: the first was that there is an obligation on professional workers to define what it is that they do—it is the study of the task which makes it professional and teachable; the second was the indefinable personal involvement of the worker in any problem that concerns people as they live, learn, grow, and relate to one another.

I was well aware that these and similar themes were in the minds of many of the colleagues with whom I had worked, and that the ideas grew when they were being shared. Part of the problem that engaged me was that the original opposing themes were matched by another opposition, viz, the harder that one tries to wrest a few certainties from the complexities of living, the greater becomes the number of uncertainties that remain. In the particular example of the mental processes, notwithstanding Freud's dictum "Where Id was, Ego shall be", it became obvious (if we accept the idea that the unconscious is infinite) that, however much the ego is enlarged, the id is undiminished.

One of the benefits of collaboration is that an idea can be put forward, shared, developed, and be brought back in a different shape. A pleasing aspect of my collaboration with Elspeth Earle was that we began this book when I was coming to the end of one of a sequence of post-retirement commitments and when she was preparing for her first consultant appointment. The book thus represents a bridge between two generations of psychiatrists, and also gives recognition to the incompleteness of any of the ideas which we use.

If we were beginning the book now we would have written it differently. In that sense it resembles the way in which our practical work develops: we start with the perception of a problem, we do something about it, and then we study what it is that we have done. The next step is to ask what would have been the result if we had done it differently. In that way we give ourselves a choice for the next occasion.

One looks back in order to be able to look forward to a future which can look after itself; and there is something of this pattern in family relationships, in teaching, and in treating some of the disorders and dissatisfactions of life.

Elspeth Earle and I approached these issues as psychiatrists, but with the knowledge that any problem with which we deal is also the proper concern of parents, of teachers, of social workers, of family doctors, and of a host of professional and voluntary workers in a variety of services and organizations.

We needed a unifying formulation which would carry the message to the reader, whether professional or non-professional. After considerable discussion, Elspeth Earle suggested using the phrase "The Cry for Help", and this allowed us to examine the ways in which a response could be made. With some deliberation, we added to the title "and the Professional Response", because our particular purpose was to discuss the way in which the response can be subjected to the discipline of study, thereby making it possible for the response to be repeatable and teachable. We do not exclude the spontaneous response, whether coming from professional or laypersons. We would add, though, that these spontaneous responses also can be recollected, and fitted, at a later date, into some concept or, alternatively, become part of a personal ethos.

Each response is an interpretation of the complaint. One approach might be to seek the cause in order to find the cure; another is to explore the meanings and purposes of the complaint or behaviour which comes to our notice.

At times the worker becomes a mediator between someone in need and the provisions which are available. Sometimes the mediation is between individuals in family or other groups. Yet again, the worker is the mediator between opposing sides in a conflict which is within an individual personality.

The title "The Cry for Help" is not without disadvantages. The phrase was first used (we have not been able to discover by whom) to refer to behaviour which calls for attention in an unfavourable way. Help may, in fact, be denied just because it seemed to be demanded. We can say, however, in Stoppard's words: "But it *was* a cry for help."

More positively, the notion of the cry for help can refer to that stage in a person's distress before any diagnosis has been made, and before any particular approach has been decided upon.

We made no attempt to keep the phrase in the forefront of our minds all the time. In some chapters of this book we allowed some theoretical and practical topics to gather their own momentum. The two original pre-occupations remain, and we have tried to chart the different frames of reference in which diseases, disorders, and dissatisfactions are experienced and dealt with.

Emphatically we do not offer any guide as to which particular framework is suited to a particular complaint or condition. Rather do we assert that whatever framework is chosen, alternatives are available and might have been chosen instead. The worker can turn aside momentarily from the task and ask what would have been the effect with a different choice.

Thus, for ourselves, we are aware of the opposition between the wish, on the one hand, to define professional tasks and, on the other, to give recognition to the emotional involvement of the helper with the helped.

In the general culture of our time, this is reflected as the opposition of the material to the spiritual. In another sense it is the opposition between the scientific faith that everything will eventually become knowable (and curable) and the philosophic doubts and nihilism of Sartre and a number of existentialists.

Surprisingly, one can feel better after reading of the poetry of desolation such as *The Waste Land* by T. S. Eliot.

Some therapists have been able to enter this area of desolation, and to emerge at a new level of personal integration. The final chapter of our book deals with the help that the helper requires and does not always get. It is insufficient to say that the helper gives love, because love in its every sense is exhaustible. Solomon, in "The Song of Songs", said:

> Stay me with flagons, comfort me with apples; for I am sick of love. (A.V.
> ii. 5)

From this same source comes the thought that one may deny oneself the care that one gives to others:

> ... they made me the keeper of the vineyards; but mine own vineyard have
> I not kept. (A.V. i. 6)

The image of cultivation is an apt one, both for the work itself and for its effects on the growth of personality of the helper and the helped.

Alternative images can be found in the area of artistic creation concerning which T. S. Eliot referred to "wholly new attempts" and "new kinds of failure". There is a creative aspect of professional work with human problems, and those who have chosen to extend and to go beyond traditional boundaries (and these include voluntary workers as well as those in established professions) have no reason to apologize for the occasions when their best efforts are not rewarded with success.

JACK KAHN

Contents

Introduction

THE term "a cry for help" was invented to call attention to the fact that people in need are not necessarily the best advocates for themselves. Attempts to gain help often defeat their object and alienate members of professions to whom people are accustomed to turn. The cry for help does not always bring help to the caller. And yet, there are many public services in which members take pride in calling themselves the "helping professions".

This book is aimed at helping the helping professions—doctors (particularly general practitioners and psychiatrists), social workers, probation officers, teachers, ministers of religion, and others—to find new frameworks of understanding within which help can be offered.

At one level we might say that disordered or unpleasant behaviour should be dealt with on its own merits. At another level we can ask what lies behind the behaviour and thereupon find more effective ways of expressing and dealing with some disturbance in the life of an individual or family.

We maintain that there cannot be either a standard response or a correct response; all we ask is that when a choice of methods is made, one should be aware of which dimension has been entered into and which aspects of the problem have been ignored. Dissatisfaction is most likely to occur where the choice has been made without consideration, or even awareness, of possible alternatives.

In some cases, however, the professional helper seems to have no option because the training and authorization offer a single approach. The implication is that doctors treat illness, teachers teach, social workers deal with personal reactions to social conditions, and that the legal structure exists in order to deter or punish infringements of the laws.

No professional work is as simple as that, nor is it confined to such boundaries. The medical profession, for example, has authorization for the treatment of illness, but doctors are consulted for (and respond to) problems that deal with the bringing up of children, marital relationships, occupational problems and the whole range of ways in which people try to respond to the human and physical environment. The same applies now to teachers and social workers. In fact, every profession is under pressure to deal with a host of problems which go far beyond the scope of traditional professional training.

There is an ethical problem too—the conflict between the principle of personal autonomy and that of responsibility of the community for its members. If, for example, a person threatens suicide, is it someone's duty to "treat" the inner distress as if it were an illness, or is there an inalienable right for any individual to decide his or her fate? Likewise, if someone threatens the person or possessions of another individual, should one look for causes or confine intervention to the observed behaviour?

The purpose of this book is to add a little complexity to many events which have been seen in too simple a way. We make the point that there are many ways of perceiving events, each with its different consequences for action. We are, therefore, providing an account of additional frames of reference in which anomalies of behaviour and experience can be perceived.

A current issue is the relationship between helper and helped. It is always an unequal relationship if one individual comes to another in order to seek help and receives it. What bothers a number of people is the question of power which is either given to, or assumed by, the helper. Ian Kennedy in the 1980 Reith Lectures seems to have fallen into the trap of assuming, particularly in relation to the medical profession, that somehow this power is institutionalized by doctors and used arbitrarily. This theme is inherent in his discussion of the nature of illness. He distinguishes between illness, which "consists first in the existence of certain physical conditions (or whatever is deemed relevant in the case of mental illness)". He regards this as a matter of objective fact which he calls a first-order judgement. In a second-order judgement, "The criteria have to do with social and moral evaluation, not perceptions of that agreed to be objective reality. The judgement is not a matter of common agreement. It is one of which doctors have made themselves and been accepted as the sole arbiters."

We on our part would contest, first of all, that illness, even of the first order of judgement, is a simple matter of physical realities—moral and social values enter into the experience of any illness, even physical.

The nature of treatment is a consequence of the particular dimension in which the illness is perceived by "the patient" and by others. Furthermore, in matters in which physical factors seem to play very little part it is simply not true that "the notion of illness has become the preserve of doctors". Whoever is consulted (whether it be doctor, social worker, spiritual advisor, or other) comes in by invitation and the response can be used or refused—unless it be a matter where the law brings in compulsion within its own structure.

To complicate the matter further, in everything except the acute illnesses (where all other activities are in suspense) an individual is a patient, pupil, or worker, and a member of a family group and of the community at one and the same time. No-one is entrusted with the exclusive responsibility for what happens next.

The power of the various professions, nevertheless, is not entirely illusory, and a challenge to real power has come from a succession of critics of medical, social work, and teaching practice. Beyond the legal obligations, which bind the professions as much as they constrain the public generally, there are more vague and more threatening aspects of the unequal relationship of expert and layman. Each profession acquires, or has thrust upon it, an authoritarian role which can be the basis of reciprocal seduction and exploitation. Challenges and criticisms, even when well founded on some point of fact, inevitably omit some component of the complex relationship. We shall have to turn to studies of transference to find reason among these irrationalities. We shall not, in the meantime, allow this issue to turn us from the duty to make the best available response to a cry for help.

Our book is intended to illustrate some of the dimensions in which disease is experienced, some of the ways in which it is perceived, and some of the ways (inadequate though they may be) in which help is provided.

1

The Cry for Help

THERE are many statements which, when first used, give a startling new perspective and which become the starting-point for progress in medical and social services. Sometimes, however, these statements degenerate, by usage, into clichés in which meaning is lost or a meaning assumed which the circumstances do not warrant. Such a fate has overcome the use of the phrase "a cry for help" when it is applied to behaviour.

The understanding of a cry for help is coloured by the shifting boundary of language usage between the professions and those whom they aim to help. The interpretation of behaviour as a cry for help was an interpretation first made by the professions, but it has now moved from professional discussions into general parlance.

It was with some reluctance that the term "cry for help" was taken as the title of this book, because, by now, the phrase is more likely to be used ironically than as a sincere interpretation. In this sense it has come to resemble the term "attention seeking", which is often taken to mean that attention should *not* be given. Thus the use of a label begins to have an effect which is exactly opposite to the effect originally attached to the phrase when newly minted.

Giving or Denying Help

There seem to be two possible responses to meet the cry for help—to give help or to ignore the cry. To some people it would seem to be a virtue that any request should be met with a denial, others feel impelled

1

to meet every demand however unreasonable. It is our purpose to look behind the superficiality in both the request and the response, and to construct a framework in which a response can be made in a professional setting.

Help is not a monopoly of the professional services. Help is given (or denied) at all levels of human interaction: in the family, in the neighbourhood, and in the community. Professional services are, or should be, distinguished by discrimination, which is another word for diagnosis.

The phrase "a cry for help" came into being when current systems of diagnosis seemed to exclude an essential message in the actions of those for whom professional services were set up. To go to the doctor one has to be ill, and therefore to disclose symptoms of illness. To go to a social service department one has to express some category of need. One could further say that in order to go to school one is expected to show a desire to learn. The relationship is clear: one party has a need, the other the resources or skill to fulfil it.

Hidden Messages

In many instances, however, the prospective patient, client, or pupil gives a message which challenges the whole ethos of the professional worker, or, for that matter, the whole ethos of society.

The continuation of a professional relationship may then depend upon the assumption that there are hidden messages in behaviour, and that there are needs for which no direct indication can be given. The term "cry for help" thus imposes a new call upon professional services, to provide some response which, up to the present, formed no part of professional training. A poignant example is the frequency with which young people are admitted to hospital after having taken overdoses of tranquillizing or pain-killing drugs which are so readily prescribed for symptoms of anxiety and distress to another member of the family. The first need is to save life by traditional medical and nursing procedures—stomach washouts, and resuscitation procedures sometimes involving the whole resources of an intensive care unit. There are further needs, but it has to be recognized that, even with modern advances in psychiatry and social work, it is the exception rather than the rule for this to be followed by really adequate enquiry into the circumstances prior to the taking of these drugs. In many cases it is only a token investigation, and, in many others, workers are only too readily prepared to accept claims from the patient that, although there has been trouble, all is now well. The worker asks for reassurance and the patient gives it.

There are other examples where the behaviour is not self-destructive but is destructive of others, and here again the response (whether in a legal framework or in some other professional setting) may be to deal with immediate circumstances and to ignore any possible indirect communication of needs. We cannot assume that it is possible, or even appropriate, always to elucidate the whole range of factors leading up to some particular act. There is a danger that a wish to go further into the sources of behaviour could become an alternative "routine" which does insufficient justice to the dangers and destructiveness of what is happening in the present. If, therefore, we use the words "cry for help" it is still necessary to be discriminating regarding the kind of intervention, if any, which is to be undertaken.

It has further to be recognized that the term "cry for help" is an interpretation, and that any interpretation is incomplete, necessarily dealing with some particular perceived aspect.

Hearing the Cry

A "cry for help" is effective when there is someone present to hear the cry and help is available. This help, however, may or may not be what is expected, and may or may not be welcome.

At least two people are concerned. One seeks help, even if only indirectly, and the other provides it. Then only is it possible for satisfactory work to be carried out. But behaviour which is interpreted as a cry for help might also be interpreted in other ways. One should not immediately conclude that behaviour is a substitute for feelings for which the person can find no other expression. In many cases, disturbing behaviour comes from someone who himself does not appear disturbed, and the disturbing effect on others may be deliberately intended and accurately directed.

No one has the right to say, "My behaviour is a cry for help." A person who gives that message should also be capable of crying, "Help", and thus not need to give signals in the form of unsatisfactory behaviour. The term "cry for help" should remain as an interpretation which comes from an examination of the individual and of the circumstances of the behaviour to which attention is being called.

Thus the phrase is used by a *person*, in a *context*, for a *purpose*, and *on behalf* of *someone else*. It is a statement *about* behaviour, and is an alternative to condemnation when the behaviour seems out of line with what is expectable or acceptable. Although the phrase cannot be used properly by the one from whom the behaviour stems, it can appropriately be used by a member of one of the primary professions, such as teaching, nursing, or general medical practice, in which there is direct contact with an unselected general population. The use has spread appropriately to the staff of material social services dealing with finance, housing, etc. and professions which carry out specialized tasks as in law and accountancy, and maybe used also by a neighbour or a family member.

Extending the Area of Professional Work

The cry for help thus becomes a way of extending the area in which a professional relationship can be offered. Bad behaviour is outside the range of professional work until a way can be found of giving a meaning to it other than badness. The interpretation allows a constructive response either directly or through referral to a specialized remedial service which is supposed to have skill in understanding hidden meanings.

Members of "the helping profession" thus have a vested interest in this kind of interpretation. Without it their own response to undesirable behaviour is that of the general public. With this interpretation there is pressure to find the meaning of bad behaviour rather than to condemn it.

The interpretation of a cry for help is usually a secondary response. The first point of contact is that of a professional worker with someone whose "bad" behaviour has given rise for concern. The professional worker has been asked to deal with it but is dissatisfied with the traditional response to the bad behaviour. He does not know how to "treat" bad behaviour, yet there are circumstances in which to punish bad behaviour offers no solution (other than relieving someone's feelings). The term "cry for help" applied to the behaviour is the answer to the cry for help that comes from the professional worker.

Thus when the worker's skills and knowledge seem to have been made useless, the term "cry for help" restores his status and self-esteem. It confirms the need that people have of his service. The helper has the need to be needed and the label of behaviour as a cry for help is a way of conserving this need.

The next level to be considered is when the professional worker of the first encounter, who attaches the label "a cry for help", passes that interpretation on to another professional service which is expected to provide the help. At this secondary stage the worker at the second point of contact may not be ready to accept a referral on these terms. His service may be no better equipped to offer appropriate help than the primary service. Here the immediate two-person relationship is between referring agent and member of a specialized service.

These themes refer particularly to referrals to the psychiatric, social work, or counselling professions, any of which may form a secondary service. A new direct relationship is formed with patient or client, but there is a need for a continuing relationship with the primary service which was first approached. If the specialized professions refuse the referral and decide that bad behaviour must be labelled for what it is, then the implication is that the presumed patient or client must take the consequences of his behaviour.

The issue is not simple. Bad behaviour is not the equivalent of an illness for which a patient may receive individual treatment, because it may have consequences for other people. Some action other than "treatment" may be called for in the interests of the others who are concerned. If a child's behaviour is troublesome either at home or at school, it is expected, in the first place, that the behaviour can be dealt with in its own setting. Failure to deal with it there leads to referral elsewhere. If the referral is to a psychiatric service, hopes are raised that the behaviour equals illness and that treatment equals cure.

The psychiatric service and (by association) the school psychological service and social service departments are believed to claim a skill in dealing with "illnesses" of this kind. The descriptive words such as "disturbance", "maladjustment", or even "difficulties" are used as if they were the equivalents of a diagnosis of a condition for which there is a cure. Consternation is caused whenever these specialized services disclaim skill in, or relevance to, some examples of disturbing behaviour.

The Value of Value Judgements

At this point we must take into account the idea that progress has been made by turning from measures which punish, or remove a person from school, home, or community, to those measures which aim to cure. Moreover, work with emotional and mental disorders is expected to absorb the standards that have grown over the years in the treatment of physical illness. The doctor does not moralize or condemn: he treats the condition from which the patient suffers. It is claimed that it is of no immediate consequence to the doctor that venereal disease may have been contracted in illicit sexual activity: the job of the doctor is to provide treatment for the condition. Similarly, in those who are called upon to treat anything which is called a disturbance of thought, feelings and behaviour are expected to be non-judgemental; in particular, they are expected to avoid value judgements, not to impose any set of ideologies which relate to social class or conventional moralities, and to accept the prospective patients or clients at the point where they now stand. The pressure to avoid value judgements in terms of descriptions of behaviour as good or bad has resulted in our taking the value judgement into ourselves. If we regard bad behaviour as illness to be cured, we, on our part, are good. If we leave it labelled as badness, it is we who are bad. Moreover, these value judgements which we attach to ourselves affect the professional image. If behaviour is labelled as bad (and not ill or mad), then we have nothing to offer as professionals. Communication has to be maintained between the helper and those whom the helper seeks to help. This is no field for those who seek an exact equation between behaviour and meaning—there is a danger of putting a general interpretation onto a piece of behaviour which may have a specific symbolism for the particular individual. To return to the example of taking an overdose, there is no universal meaning to be attached to the act. If the bottle says, "Take two tablets—it is dangerous to exceed the dose", then a person who takes four tablets (double the dose) may not be making an unambiguous "cry for help", but may be wishing to kill either the pain or himself. In an indirect way this might still enclose a cry for help. It is important to listen to what the patient has to say. Even when a massive dose of the tablets has been taken, there may still be doubts as to whether this was done with a hope that life may be saved after all, together with the gaining of an appreciation (previously lacking) of the state of distress which had been reached.

We have already referred to situations in which a willing helper makes contact with a person who only reluctantly accepts help, and also to cases where the behaviour is an undisguised "cry for help", or even more plainly an importunate demand. In these latter cases, more than in any other, we should be clear about what we have to offer. If we can neither carry out the demands that are made by others, nor fulfil the needs as we ourselves see them, then the best service we can offer is the honesty of our approach. The turning of our response into effective help requires some judgement about the implications and effects of the behaviour, and requires some possibility that the person concerned has the capacity to understand his responsibility for the behaviour. Furthermore, he should be willing to find *alternative* forms of expression. The successful treatment gives an increase in repertoires of behaviour and attaches responsibility of choice. There is behaviour which may be described as bad or destructive by others but which is quite satisfying to the person concerned. To label it as a "cry for help", and to give a benign interpretation to it, carries a danger of collusions in which a badly behaved person is given the role of patient. This allows him to abdicate all personal responsibility for his actions. If it necessarily becomes someone else's professional task to treat him as a patient, his continued misdeeds would then have to be accepted as a failure of his treatment rather than as his own failure.

The helper has already taken value judgements of goodness and badness into himself instead of applying them to the "patient". Next he removes the idea of *guilt* as properly attaching to undesirable beha- viour, and takes that also into himself. If the patient complains of the burden of "guilt feelings", the helper feels guilty in that he has been neither skilful nor good enough to provide the help that he thinks is required. The phrase "guilt feelings" is used to relieve the patient of appropriate feelings of guilt.

The Treatment Barrier

R. D. Scott[1] describes a *treatment barrier* which occurs by the very labelling of a person as "a mental patient" by a doctor or some other authority. Once this happens it is assumed that the whole of his behaviour is an aspect of the illness and that therefore the responsibility for the behaviour belongs to the doctor who is treating the illness. Scott cites the example of a patient from a mental hospital who goes out for the day and creates trouble in the neighbouring town—picks a fight, upsets a shopkeeper or a bus conductor. When this citizen complains directly or through the police, "the patient" says: "I'm from such-and-such a hospital" (mental hospital). The hospital doctor is phoned and held totally responsible for this person, who, because he is a mental patient, is assumed not to be responsible for his own behaviour. If the doctor does not take this view, and acts accordingly, then the community member maybe angry with the doctor and may threaten to report him to a higher authority. But if the doctor *does* take this view, there is little chance of effectively changing the behaviour of the patient. The explanation of the behaviour as being a feature of mental illness becomes a treatment barrier and not an aid to treatment. Scott suggests that the treatment barrier can be broken down by asking the patient a few simple questions: "Why are you here?", "What has happened?", "Are you ill?", "Is there anything for which you would like help?" According to Scott there are a number of attributes which are attached to the mental patient by the public, and most patients, wittingly or unwittingly, fulfil those characteristics. They are: to have a tendency not to be responsible; to have no volition to determine their own fate; to have a tendency to avoid committing themselves; and to be without insight into their own behaviour. At this point we should recognize that the attribution of "a cry for help", which can be applied to people living and working in the community (as well as to patients in hospital), is an application of these same attributes.

At this level of formulation the cry for help negates the notion of effectiveness of treatment. It would become a complete explanation of the behaviour and a removal of responsibility for it, rather than lead to

---

[1] SCOTT, R. D., The treatment barrier, Part 2L, *Br. J. med. Psychol.* **46**, 45; (1973). Part 2, The patient as an unrecognised agent, *Br. J. med. Psychol.* **46**, 57 (1973).

a conscious choice of alternative forms of behaviour less disturbing to others. *The term "cry for help" is useful when it leads to efforts in which the prospective patient takes a share in arriving at conclusions that lead to change.*

There is, however, another cry for help which is not really a cry for actual help to be given, but is a cry to be heard. This is the need for attention which only too often leads the person who hears the cry to conclude that attention should not be given. We have mentioned the reluctance to give attention to those who demand it; some people fear that the bad behaviour will be reinforced. If a psychiatrist writes in his report about a child, "This is *attention-seeking* behaviour", it is immediately assumed that the child should not be given attention and should be ignored. If the psychiatrist merely alters his phrasing, "This is *attention-needing* behaviour", the parent or teacher feels justified in listening to the communication made via the behaviour. But constantly there is the fear that the child or patient is making demands that are unreasonable or unrealizable. There are indeed those who are insatiable and whose demands are inordinate, and the intensity of the cry increases with each inevitable failure to gain a response. Such a person is not "cured" by withholding all responses, but neither is it a satisfactory form of interpretation to imply that the helper should have an infinite capacity to give. The cry for help, and its response, is, in general, thought of as emitting from those who have in the past received at least an approximation of their needs, and where there is a possibility that some adjustments can be made to relative failures to receive the supply of some particular provision. The assumption is that adjustment will be made, either by supplying something of that which has been missing or perhaps curing that which has gone wrong.

In some cases the deficiency is major and goes deep into the structure of the personality. There are those who acquire the label of "criminal", or "psychopath", and some who acquire a bad prognostic clinical label such as "paranoid". There are also those whose behaviour appears to be capricious and not traceable sequentially to underlying causes.

The message of the behaviour may be haphazard and part of a series of failures to achieve coherent relationships. The behaviour may be part of the almost random responses to factors in the network of interpersonal relationships. Hope in these cases does not lie in any remedial process, but rather in the possibility of small gains from compensatory beneficial experiences that are granted without any condition that behaviour must change.

Entitlements to Help

Help, so far, has not been defined. It is assumed that psychiatric and personal social services are in possession of something which can be offered to people in distress, even when the distress is expressed in some form of disguise. Those with physical illnesses do not need to have their messages translated. Neither do those with clearly recognizable deficiencies of material needs. The physical illness is "admission" to a doctor's surgery; the material need, to some of the services of the welfare state. The general practitioner who knows the patient and his previous personality and illness pattern is in a good position to decipher the illness and help the patient to understand himself. In addition, the G.P. may have sufficient insight and influence over the patient to perceive a lack and put it right while treating some illness. For example, a person who attends surgery with abdominal pain may mention financial difficulties, and the G.P. can arrange for a social worker to visit the patient at home. The applicant for social security or rehousing has a material need for which help is sought, and there may be another need (emotional) which becomes understandable to the experienced and sensitive officer. Likewise, a clue to some physical illness may be given by the applicant for some material service or one receiving casework in a social work agency.

The identification of emotional distress should not divert the attention of the primary professional worker (or welfare officer or any other profession) from the reality of the original request. The awareness of the emotional component may lead to referral elsewhere, or an appropriate response to it may become part of the original officer's skill. When someone turns to a doctor, he becomes a patient. When he is ill, he receives help; therefore there may be some who become ill in order to get help. There may be others who are able to concentrate on physical and financial circumstances (because these also give an entitlement to be heard) rather than complain about fears and anxiety.

It does not necessarily follow that those who have mental symptoms should have mental treatment. A paranoid individual may complain that other people influence his thoughts and read his mind, and he makes it plain that his destructive behaviour is a response to imagined influence of other people. Such an individual, who would steadfastly deny he was mentally ill (but merely suffering from intrusion by others), can receive benefit from a doctor who treats his physical condition and from a social worker who finds some help for his circumstances of living. There is a further benefit which comes indirectly from the experience of goodness in the outside world. Paradoxically, the psychiatrist who attempts to interpret the mental process may merely confirm the patient in his delusion that he is being persecuted by people with power to enter his thoughts.

Every professional worker has limits to his skill which derive from his personality, training, and experience. Professions have their boundaries, but members learn to go to some extent beyond them. It is necessary to recognize that problems may go beyond the worker's authorization. It may be necessary, on these occasions, for the worker to point out this situation to the client. Treatment that goes beyond traditional boundaries may also go beyond what the patient has bargained for. And yet many patients accept what might seem to be an unwarranted intrusion into their affairs, so long as they gain their original demand. The worker should refuse to become involved in a so-called "treatment programme" in which a search is made for underlying causes in mental functioning unless the client is willing and able to co-operate with exploration into areas of which he may not yet be aware. Thus, even if we understand the cry for help, we may not be able to satisfy it, nor do we always have authorization to make this attempt; the professional should not feel that he has to respond to every call and provide an answer.

Just as a mother will go to her crying infant and try to understand the needs but cannot always provide the necessary comfort, so also do workers in the professional fields of psychiatry and social work have sometimes to listen to the cry of those clients who may cry in vain.

2
Notions of Help

Institutionalization of Help

In referring to the helper's response to the cry for help we have to look at the helper's own self. The helper answers the demand that an individual makes either for the relief of acute distress or for long-term provision of the requirements for that individual's development.

When the professional response fits in with some common ideology of the community (or a section of it), the help becomes institutionalized in the work of different professions—medicine, social work, and teaching. The individual professional worker's response is no longer a private response, but is under the umbrella of the appropriate professional service which claims the ownership of a body of professional knowledge, an authorization, and a standardized training. There is further an implicit agreement from the community that help should be offered even to those who are not directly asking for it, but whose behaviour or circumstances imply that they require it.

Historically the personal physician had a responsibility exclusively to his patient, and the relationship was akin to that of the individual and priest, who was healer, teacher, and pastor all at the same time. Behind this relationship the helper derived support from an ideological or spiritual belief. The work of the modern doctor is only in part an inheritance from this, as he now often works in a team with other professionals. The social worker's task too has changed in the last century. The work has moved from provision of material assistance to the deprived and has been extended to the concern for any member of the community in times of vulnerability. The teacher, who is now part of an intricate educational system, has taken on functions that are more complex than the mere transmission of knowledge. Teachers are acknowledged also as interpreters of ideas regarding ways of life which are handed down as part of the continuity of the educational system.

The vagueness of the word "help" has come to the rescue of those who find it necessary to extend and enlarge their previous notions of professional activities. It is the word "help" that brings medical services, educational services, and social services coincidentally to one and the same problem. The same vagueness accompanies ideas of what is to be done, for whom it has to be done, and who it is that has to do it. It is therefore necessary to take some of the traditional ideas from every profession and to attempt to trace how people unwittingly step out of one frame of reference into another. The ideas of curing, and of providing for development, and of arranging for supplies of material needs have also had to become subservient at times to ideas about the processes of interaction between individuals in their different groupings. Knowledge which no longer belongs exclusively to single professions is accumulating. Even where exciting new ideas have been created, and have been used effectively, there still may be doubt about the appropriate choice out of many alternatives. There is uncertainty about the place of any one particular process in the general background of provision for the needs of individuals and families. For example, one need only look at the widespread enthusiasm for family therapy, and for close-encounter groups, to recognize that some procedures are created within the confines of a single profession and that they spread to other professions and the laity. Conversely, there are ideas which start with the gifted amateur, the far-sighted administrator, and sometimes with the false prophet, that get taken up by the professional worker. The runaway enthusiast is likely to turn a brilliant innovation into the promise of a panacea, with inevitable disillusionment. Each new discovery increases the problem of having to discriminate between available methods in order to find one that is suitable and available. This is the question of what it is that has to be done, for whom, and by whom.

The most pressing contemporary need is for a comprehensive chart of reference which will encompass the different kinds of work at present being professionally undertaken. Each worker needs to be aware of alternative frames of reference which *might* have been chosen, and which, in fact, may actually be being entered into unbeknown to him by other workers at one and the same time. In a later chapter we shall give a list of the frames of reference that we have chosen in order to differentiate some of the different activities with which we are familiar. We shall follow this with more detailed description of each separate frame.

Underlying the move from established models of working within a single profession towards an exploration of areas of common interest is the move from certainty to uncertainty, and cherished traditions have to be challenged.

In medicine, for example, the work which carries the highest esteem is that based on diagnosis. The academic ideal is a search for hard clinical facts which can be objectively observed, measured, and recorded. The findings become the material of research in which sound methodology will permit other observers to repeat the observations in order to confirm or refute the original findings. Nevertheless, doctors in general, and psychiatrists in particular, have been faced with problems which cannot be made to fit into the idealized pattern of diagnosis. Many clinicians have not hesitated to step out of the area of certainty and to enter into areas which are on the fringe of existing knowledge.

At the same time, workers in other professions have, conversely, shown a tendency, when dealing with problems of human relationships and with the quality of the provisions for living, to turn towards a diagnostic approach. They have attempted to transpose the medical model, with its certainties, into a system for finding some finality even in those areas in which value systems continue to prevail. The familiar questions are: What is it? What has caused it? How do we recognize it? How do we treat it? These questions are asked, and an answer is confidently assumed to be available, in relation to unhappiness, inadequacy, bad behaviour, and a failure to receive the current entitlements of a member of a particular community.

Searching for Certainty

The temptation to find certainty is sometimes so strong, and the discomfort of uncertainty so great, that many workers may prefer to hold onto traditional views even when they have become inadequate. Other workers hurry through the uncertainties towards a prematurely formulated new dogma which is no more adequate than the old. The most difficult task of all is to hold onto the uncertainty while it is still being creative. Conflicting ideologies, stoutly maintained, probably contain a good deal of both error and shrewd thinking.

The redefinition of a problem is a form of interpretation. Something new is substituted for the customary answer to a routine question—bad behaviour evokes punishment until the bad behaviour is given a new meaning, and then bad behaviour apparently brings a reward or benefit. If badness equals illness, then the treatment equals benefit. Sometimes the benefits are heavily disguised and take the form of treatment which is unwelcome. In many cases of mental illness, treatment may be feared as an intrusion into the autonomy of the person who becomes an unwilling patient. A complete circle has now been turned and some professional workers, who may very well perceive the implied message of badness equals madness equals need for treatment, may yet shrink from pursuing this logic because it no longer seems kind. Badness equals treatment would be acceptable but for the fact that the treatment in this case is for a lowly esteemed category of illness, viz. mental disorder. The uncomfortable part of the treatment equation is that treatment equals madness.

In effect, the worker says to himself: "If I don't like the consequence, I won't read the message." Put another way, if one does not like the consequence in the form of treatment, one fights hard against making the diagnosis. For example, the doctor who knows his patient and hears the statement that a man has thoughts which he feels are beyond his control may not be ready to believe that the man is insane. He is not ready to set in motion the procedures which may result in admission to psychiatric hospital. Hospital admission is thought of as worse than the sequential implications of not making a psychiatric diagnosis. It is thought to be kinder not to recognize what the patient is saying. False reassurance is given in the form: "But you wouldn't really do it, would you?" Here the doctor is really reassuring himself. The patient, too, may come for reassurance that the thoughts are of no consequence. The helper's skill consists in taking the message seriously enough and not belittling the potential patient's fears (which are real and possibly justified) without going to the other extreme of over-responding to the universal fears of the uncontrollable part of human heritage. Several examples can be given: the person who takes the opportunity of telling the doctor about the strange behaviour of a neighbour—he bangs on the communicating wall during the night, apparently in answer to delusions involving those in adjoining homes. The doctor recognizes this as psychotic and says such a person ought to be taken into hospital. Almost immediately the complaint about the neighbour may be withdrawn: "I wouldn't like to be responsible for putting him away."

Behaviour as Metaphor

At an equally serious level is the complaint that a patient makes about his or her own distress where it may be difficult to distinguish a figure of speech from an intention. "I feel like putting my head in the gas oven"—this may be a form of words in which to express the distress which is still within the bounds of toleration. If a person adds, "But of course I wouldn't really do it", it is somewhat more serious because the thought of the actuality had crossed the mind! The message is still even more complex when given in less direct ways—for example, by breaking the law in the way which creates a disturbance and draws the attention of the police. A man may take a brick and throw it at a shop window. If the police are called in it becomes recognizable on enquiry that the impetus was mental disturbance and not criminal intention. A sensitive superior officer decides not to bring any charge and contacts a social service department with responsibility for duties within the mental health services. At this stage there may be no indication of mental disorder other than the behaviour, but the opportunity to investigate the mental implications of the action has now passed. There is something to be said for those critics of psychiatric theory, such as Ivan Illich or Szasz, who deny the existence of mental illness but are ready to accept the application of legal consequences for breaking the law. One might add that the legal process can sometimes be used constructively when the offender takes the next step himself of saying, "But I was ill", and actually asking for a psychiatric consultation. It would still be necessary to distinguish between two kinds of plea of mental disturbance: one may be merely an effort to evade legal consequences of behaviour without any intention to pursue treatment; the other is a reluctant realization of mental disorder which had previously been denied.

In an actual case a man created a public disturbance and threatened to kill a neighbour; as a consequence, a policeman was brought to the scene. The behaviour was sufficiently characteristic of mental illness to be recognized as such by the policeman, and neither the neighbour nor the policeman wished to press charges. It was hoped that somehow the man would seek and find successful treatment. The family doctor was informed, but by this time the patient denied any abnormality in his thinking or behaviour.

Shortly afterwards, this man went into the cathedral of a nearby city and told one of the clergy that he intended to kill the queen. Immediately steps were taken to admit him to psychiatric hospital where he himself found safety. In this case, the message, given and withdrawn, was, "My thoughts are so strange and uncontrollable that I'm afraid I may do something dangerous." But those who read the message also wanted to protect him from the imagined and real undesirable legal consequences of his behaviour. On his own part, the man was still unable to recognize his inner distress without translating it into abnormal behaviour. This particular man was not able to go into hospital except under compulsion, and so his further message was, "Take me into hospital, even by force, because there is no limit to the damage I might do."

In the above case treatment could only be achieved by taking the step of hospital admission. The man had to be taken from his home compulsorily. And yet it is now the public policy, accepted by most professional workers, that mental disorder should be treated without all the legal and social consequences of a formal psychiatric diagnosis which at one time seemed inevitably to involve removal from home.

The modern treatment of psychiatric illness includes the use of drugs, and there is a great deal of mental disorder which no psychiatrist ever sees because it does not go beyond the family doctor's surgery. Psychiatric diagnosis is not an all-or-nothing affair. In some cases loss of control is partial and temporary, and very little is needed to restore the normal balance of mind. The understanding of a message, and an honest response to it, may be sufficient to bring the problem back into the range of what the individual himself can control. Sometimes a drug will reduce the physical effects of anxiety. At other times it is sufficient for someone to put the problem into words that do justice to the patient's distress. This is not the same as "reassurance" in the false sense of saying there is no problem. It is reassurance in the sense that the problem is within someone else's comprehension. The degree of alienation is reduced by increasing the amount of common understanding.

Some responses confirm the professional status—the doctor knows he is a doctor, and confirms his identity, when he gives a drug. If he gives an interpretation in a way which was not part of his original training, he may feel he is stepping out of his role, and thereby giving an inferior service. It may be said proudly of a doctor, "He is all right with those who are really ill, but has no time for those who come for a talk." Similarly there are teachers who say their job is just to teach, not to solve problems; and there are social workers who feel most useful to society when they identify material needs and find ways of supplying them. On the other hand, there are doctors, teachers, and social workers who look upon their highest function as that of understanding human personality in all its complexities. Their aim would be to explore and clarify problems rather than to supply some mechanistic solution.

Professional Esteem and Ideologies

A hierarchical scale of values is an important part of professional image, and the danger here is of selecting the form of treatment which confirms ideological values of individuals or of whole professions.

Individual workers, and professional services as a whole, acquire an image which influences the way in which they are used. Members of the public may select a service which fits the need of which they are most aware.

The distraught parent whose battering behaviour threatens the life of an infant may give indications to a neighbour, to a health visitor, or to the casualty department of the local hospital. Messages may be given and withdrawn at the moment they are understood, but some messages are repeated until someone really takes notice.

Non-accidental Injury

The "non-accidental injury" frequently has the far-reaching effect of removal of the baby from the parental home. This is a consequence which is easier for the medical services to contemplate than for social services departments to implement. Professional workers have absorbed the message of the importance of maternal (or paternal) contact for the normal development of the infant; consequently it is not easy to take the diametrically opposed view that the parents' contact is a threat to the life of the child. Moreover, those who have to arrange for local authority care have no illusions about variations in the quality of the substitute care which they are able to provide. It is part of their ethos that they should work with a family to maintain its integrity, even if a mother, apparently at the end of her tether, makes the contact herself and asks for her child to be taken from her and into care. Drawing upon the highest professional standards, the worker tries to maintain the child's place in the family all the more because the mother is anxious to get rid of it. In order to do this it may seem necessary to deny the reality of the violence of the parents' feelings.

When the violence finds physical expression, legal proceedings are instituted for a care order in which the infant is taken from the parents. The parent may then say, "You didn't help me by taking care of the child when I asked, and now you are doing it by force." Whatever decision is made in those circumstances, some aspect of it is unwelcome, both to the worker and to the family members. The treatment is not like that in physical medicine where it is directly related to disease, and is expected to lead to a cure. It may well be necessary to take the child from the home, but the problem of parental disharmony or disorders of the individual personalities of both parents may still remain. There may be problems of finance, housing, or jobs, and the problems may be without solutions and yet require the workers to make an effort to help.

No item in the multi-dimensional message should be unheard or left without some response. At some stage in dealing with non-accidental injury in children there may have to be a deliberate turning from a therapeutically guided response towards the parents to that of confronting the parents with the responsibility for what they themselves are doing. The serious damage to the infant has criminal implications. Treatment of the parents is not enough, especially where treatment cannot guarantee safety for the child.

There are cases where, even with severe and obvious injuries, the parents deny their part in the production of them. No "treatment" in these circumstances can be effective, either to clarify the situation for the parents' own sake or to afford safety for the child who is part of the family distress.

Those who work in a therapeutic setting may be skilled in asking questions about feelings that bring unexpected answers and which ultimately can be turned to a therapeutic purpose. They are not so skilled at confronting people with questions of fact which lead to admissions of guilt, with adverse consequences within the system of enforcement of the law. An inquisitorial approach may in some cases have to precede any attempts at effective therapy either for the individuals or for the family as a whole. No one can treat what is said not to exist. This is where the police may have to be informed in order to use the skills of police interviews to ascertain the facts which have to be dealt with. This again brings in an aspect of compulsion which is unwelcome to those who prefer to see all their work as satisfying the desires, as well as the needs, of those with whom they work. When damage has been done, and acknowledged, there may still be room for an interpersonal approach which goes along with responsibility for future rather than past conduct. Within this field, the interpretative work of dynamically orientated workers in psychiatry and in social work has to supplement the statutory services which include the police and the National Society for Prevention of Cruelty to Children.

There are two complementary principles: the need to safeguard the vulnerable and the hope of reaching the unconscious roots of the behaviour of those responsible for the danger. For the first there are clearly laid down procedures within the law; for the second we turn, sometimes too optimistically, to therapeutic services. There has been the belief that if we identify unconscious motives for behaviour we can eradicate any aspect of it that is undesirable. It is essential, therefore, to realize that there are problems that are beyond the prospective patient's control, and that there are problems beyond the capacity of the professional helper. Compulsory external preventative measures, however unwelcome they may be, are necessary.

Those who believe that whenever there is a problem of behaviour a solution can be found through understanding may build up a relationship with patients in which there is a shared fantasy that the worker "does" and the patient is "done to".

It seems all too easy to see what is wrong with someone's life, whether it be early deprivation or poor conditions under which a family lives, but it is all so difficult to make reparation for these early deprivations. Those who feel that whatever was missed during childhood can be replaced if enough love and care is given will have some rewarding successes and some despairing failures.

There is an aspect of interpretation where the skill of the worker is to bring into being an unexpected and unfamiliar perspective to the vision of the client. The same must apply to the worker's own perceptions. It is a new skill to see bad behaviour as something which is a cry for help and a call on the professional worker to come to some individual's aid. The next level is to turn this round again and to recognize the complexities of messages where the behaviour also has to be taken on its own merits, even if the consequences appear to be adverse and imply a return to traditional values. The return, however, is not full circle: new levels of understanding can be incorporated into the old. It is important for the worker, who brings the process of confrontation to the client, not to be himself repelled by an adverse response to his best efforts. There are many workers who are able to remain in contact with the most unlikely individuals and families and continue to work without any reward or any apparent change in their behaviour. In many such cases, however, the best result possible may be a slow accumulation of small gains, and yet even this does not come if it is looked for as a condition of the continuation of the worker's interest. It is not given to every worker, nor should it be demanded, to love the "unlovable".

There are some who have this special quality. For the vast majority of professional workers, professional standards are the protection for the client that ensure that the service never goes below a level which offers consideration and respect even when approval cannot be given.

3
Whence Cometh My Help?

AT FIRST sight of it would seem reasonable to assume that the nature of help would be decided on the basis of the kind of problem for which help is being sought. It seems to us that help more frequently becomes shaped by the person (or organization) with whom the first contact happens to be made. Help is thus structured by persons, professions, and organizations; and the problem itself is seen in the image of the help which is at hand. Some organizations have come into existence in order to make available help of a kind that did not previously exist. Some are set up to deal with a category of disaster, or with a problem of people at some particular stage of life, or to represent a professional ideology which appears to offer solution for distress.

Categories of Institution

Grunebaum[1] has categorized types of institution offering help and sets out these categories against a background of social organization within the community as a whole. His first theme is, therefore, the level at which problems arise and the level at which interventions occur.

Grunebaum sees psychological dysfunction as occurring at the level either of the individual or of the family, but he takes in other considerations such as neighbourhood or catchment area.

Turning to institutions, he enumerates the professional, organizational, and functional components.

[1] GRUNEBAUM, HENRY (ed.), *The Practice of Community Mental Helath*, Little, Brown & Co., Boston, 1970.

CFH 3*

The following headings are taken from Grunebaum, with some slight modifications of our own.

(1) Institutions treating particular problem areas, e.g. delinquency, alcoholism, drug addiction. These bring together those workers who have become interested in treating some particular facets of behaviour, and they may well go on to discover a diversity of underlying pathology or causation under the initial single heading.

(2) Institutions treating particular age groups, e.g. infant welfare clinics, adolescent units, geriatric services.

(3) Institutions using specialized therapeutic approaches, e.g. psychoanalysis, counselling, behaviour therapy, and, we would now add, family therapy.

Any client or patient referred to and accepted by any such organization is prepared at the beginning for the kind of response that will be offered.

(4) Institutions using the label of traditional hospital departments, e.g. in-patient unit, out-patient unit, day hospital, occupational centres.

(5) Institutions emphasizing the level of social organization of the clients, e.g. individual therapy, group therapy, marital therapy, and therapeutic communities.

It will be seen that some of these overlap, and many types of organization have escaped the above categorization. For example, there are issues which affect staffing. Do workers prefer to deal with special problems at a high level of skill, or to cover a wide range of problems in order not to exclude some of the individuals who approach the service?

The theme of specialism versus generalization affects the training recruitment and the images in which the workers are perceived. Alongside this is the career structure which may either recognize promotion in clinical functions with increasing qualifications and experience or, alternatively, promotion may lead to advancement within the administrative structure of an organization. In the latter case the worker who is promoted virtually changes the professional role and sometimes begins work for which he has been given no training and, possibly, for which he even has no aptitude.

Single- and Multi-professional Services

Beyond all this there is another main division of services to which we wish to call attention—the single profession as against a multi-disciplinary service. As examples of single-professional services we could instance the probation services and the former child care services and its successor, the social service departments. Educational psychology is a single-professional service when working purely within the schools, but a part of a multi-disciplinary service when working within, or together with, the child guidance clinic. General medicine began as a single-professional service and gradually extended its role through the use of ancillary and subordinate services.

Medical services have become doubly complicated. First there is the increasing specialism within medicine, where practitioners may work independently on the problems referred to them or in co-ordination with other specialists. Doctors in different specialities may not share anything beyond their first qualification: they have different postgraduate experience, read different journals, and acquire a language which is almost unintelligible to anyone outside the speciality. Yet a patient may pass from one specialist to another or require simultaneous investigation or treatment from more than one. Someone needs to be the co-ordinator, and usually it is the general practitioner who becomes a specialist in continuous care.

Secondly, professions which were formerly ancillary to medicine have developed skills and criteria of their own, and they have been able to command a share in decision-making. This not only includes nurses, physiotherapists, speech therapists, radiographers, and a host of technicians—it also includes porters, cleaners, and operatives who maintain the buildings and essential services. The alternatives to multi-disciplinary decisions seem to be repeated battles to establish dominance of some particular party at a critical moment.

Some of the industrial strife within the hospital service seems to have arisen because there are workers who have power but no voice. They do not appear to be consulted on decisions of policy unless they use their power to bring the work to a standstill.

Work with people with psychiatric disorders need not be restricted to psychiatric treatment, i.e. work not directed to the psychopathology (or any other physical or physiological conceptualization of the disorder) in someone who happens to be schizophrenic. This work, whether carried out by a psychiatrist, nurse, psychologist, social worker, or teacher, is as separate from psychiatry as the water supply, housing, and sewage works are from the health services which are provided by the medical practitioner. All these things are necessary for physical health, and we must recognize that there are functional areas of living which are necessary to mental health but are not psychiatric. We should expect changes in a broad range of services to be initiated at any point by workers within the clinical service, and by gifted administrators who shape policy, by political/social commentators, and even by the "protest groups" who agitate for provision of services for some particular problem. We should take into account the mass media, where the main purpose sometimes appears to be to entertain (or even merely to sell their product). The communicators in these media are successful when they are sensitive to areas of public concern. We are also well aware that in all these cases there may be exploitation of members of the public to promote and enhance a profession, to create and continue an organization, to increase political power, or, sometimes, merely for some financial reward.

In discussing the criteria which go to make a profession, we are brought face to face with the professional response to a cry for help. There are those who would argue that the barrier between the person who cries for help and the professional who responds should be removed.

Professional distance is maintained by reciprocal expectations—the transference and counter-transference—and by the reality of the behaviour and physical presentation of the therapist's personality. At one time the professional worker had a stylized form of dress—still maintained by lawyers when working in the courts. Within medicine, formal dress has been abandoned by many general practitioners whose lives are fairly close to the patients, but is still maintained by many specialists. Within hospital, a white coat distinguishes the doctor, and members of some other professions, from the patients in the same way as the nursing uniform identifies the provider of a particular kind of help.

Professional Distance

Many people have felt that formality and the maintenance of a professional distance is a disadvantage and a negation of the equality in the human factor of those concerned. Within psychiatry, in particular, there are units where it is a point of principle that the doctors do not wear white coats and, with a little more resistance to the change, psychiatric nurses may also wear ordinary clothing. This is a feature of therapeutic communities where the hierarchical organization in a medical setting is challenged in that it maintains stereotyped roles of patients who have to comply with the rules of residence and even with the professional image of the syndrome from which they are supposed to suffer. There is much in common in this with the image of the pupil role which is resisted by young people in the extra years since the school-leaving age has been raised.

The essential equality in the relationship is enhanced when the professional person encourages the use of first names. There is also a group tendency for professional workers to adopt the informal (and sometimes trendy) fashions in clothes of the youth culture, with a clear message that traditional barriers have been overcome. It is interesting that formal professional clothes, as in the High Courts, were the ordinary clothing of an earlier century.

There is another side to this argument. Formality and tradition can be a protection in some cases to the person seeking help. The relationship is not really equal. The helper is expected to have knowledge, skill, and, in some cases, authority. Moreover, the one seeking help comes for a problem which may be unique in the lifetime of an individual or family, and important; to the helper it may be a commonplace of the profession. A lack of formality may seem to be a denigration of the importance of the problem. In a court of law, in the doctor's surgery, or in the solicitor's and accountant's office there is an etiquette which guarantees that the service does not fall below a certain level of seriousness. Equality is not enough as the basis of a relationship for the supply of some kinds of needs. This is well exemplified when a member of a profession has a need for the kind of service that he or she is involved in. The doctor who is ill gets poor service if he is treated as a colleague and not as a patient. The psychiatrist who is mentally disturbed may pass unheeded, but not unnoticed, by his colleagues, who might not wish to presume to put him into a patient's role.

All these issues are reflected in some of the features of family life. There is a generation difference between parents and children which includes an essential inequality. Whatever the hazards of incest might be, the one certain feature is that a father who becomes his daughter's lover deprives her of his role as a father. The same process occurs with a teacher who becomes a supplicant for a pupil's love, or a seducer, or even the object of intimacy initiated by the pupil. The therapist who responds to a patient's need for physical love becomes unable to maintain any therapeutic principle which requires personal restraint on the behaviour in the patient's life in the outside world. A social worker who is addressed by his first name may have difficulty in proceeding with some statutory enforcement.

The professional worker is in the dilemma of providing the goodness of caring which occurs between parents and children, between lovers, and between friends, and which is sometimes expressed in religious terms; and yet the professional worker receives a payment in salary or fee. It is important to recognize this distinction, which often weighs heavily upon the rich who wonder whether they would be able to get help if they did not pay for it. One of the advantages to the professional worker in the public services is that he does not often have to discuss the question of payment; payment nevertheless exists. The one seeking help may have obligations through taxation, and, in addition, seeking help needs the giving of time by both parties and the acceptance of some kinds of rules, even granted that some of these may be negotiable.

However, this brings us back to the importance of diagnosis and to the choice of a frame of reference. Before there can be any intervention at a professional level we must know *what* we are "treating". Unless one has defined (and possibly redefined) the nature of the problem for which help is being sought, intervention may add to the disorder in the one seeking help. Caring is not enough, and those who advocate a less formal "humanistic" approach need also to have the ability to bring a specific skill for an identified problem.

General and Specific Help

Granted that skill, the worker's caring can then give more generalized developmental benefits that are akin to growing up and maturing in the family, in the schools, and in general adult life. This brings us back to the question of specialism versus generic training. It seems to us that there is nothing that is so specialized as general professional care in a professional setting. The general practitioner is more than a signpost to specialized services. He has to have the capacity to make a diagnosis but also to hold the knowledge about the patient's day-to-day existence, with its anomalies and illnesses. He even has to accept responsibility for continued care of the incurable who are passed in and out of the care of specialists and departments in hospital. The general practitioner has to be familiar with the process of birth and the personal and family impact of death, even where someone is a long time dying.

The social worker, too, who has a generic training is expected to be familiar with normal development, with family life, and to recognize the occasions when extra support is needed. For some anomalies it is essential to emphasize that these are the experience to some degree of everyone. There are other cases where their claim is that this person's experience is different from that of the rest of the community. The worker has to be sufficient of a specialist to be able to recognize where the difference lies.

Criteria of Professions

The criteria which go towards making a profession are:
(1) The possession of a theoretical body of knowledge;
(2) The authorization given by training, qualification, or appointment;
(3) Acceptance of discipline within a professional ethic;
(4) Authority or competence in the job;
(5) Awareness of a body of hearsay knowledge—this is an accumulation of informal knowledge about colleagues and systems relating to the work, i.e. who does what and where.

These criteria which go to make up a profession also allow an individual member of the profession to make a contract, for a purpose, with another person, or to continue an existing contract. Problems can arise, especially since the introduction of the generic social work training, for a professional worker who may have responsibility for a whole family. If he suspects that a child is at risk within that family, should the contract be with one or other parent, or with the child himself, or even with one of the siblings?

We have introduced the word "contract" at this stage in order to emphasize the difficulty of decisions regarding who is the person on whose behalf one is working. No such difficulty occurred when the individual patient approached the isolated practitioner and the whole of the treatment was an implied contract between two people. The actual conditions were tried by tradition and there was no need to specify what they were. There are now many more parties to the arrangement. The worker is part of an organization, the person requiring help is part of a social system with obligations as well as needs, and the nature of the work may be a matter of public policy as much as an attempt to satisfy personal distress.

In this sense the word "contract" may be inappropriate if neither party is truly free to negotiate what is required, in the background of what is actually available and having regard to the more nebulous notion of what is requisite. It is at this point that we recall the professional requirements of a discipline which is related to ethical values as a part of the culture in which the help and helper exist.

4

The Professional Response

IN THE preceding chapter we have made the point that help is made available in the organized work of different professions. Each profession has its separate and exclusive skills, but medicine, education, and social work also have something in common. They frequently work to the same ends by different means. Something is offered for an immediate need, but in the background there is thought for the provision of requirements of individual development.

Originally people sought satisfaction for their needs by private arrangement; help was provided for those who sought it. Gradually the primary services for health and education have been made available for the whole population. It is implicit that the whole community should have available the provisions and opportunities that the more fortunate and perceptive members arranged personally for themselves and their families.

The remedial services come first, to be followed by facilities for those who suffer from some anomaly of development or those whose performance and circumstances do not reach conventionally approved standards. There is now a community feeling that supplementary services should be offered even to those who are unaware of any form of inadequacy.

·Common Ideology

The central core of curing, teaching, and aiding belongs to all three services. Skills are defined according to category of disease for curing, stages of development for teaching, and according to measurable material deficiencies for social work. All three now include (or should include) the aim of providing for inadequacies in early nurturing, and thus "caring" is a common feature. The essential skill includes some knowledge of the way in which individuals interact with one another. The skills distinguish the professions; each profession develops its own means of assessing the requirements.

Professional Boundaries

Professions thus have been able to emphasize the boundaries of their work while developing their separate contributions. For some purposes, however, they cover the same ground. Each profession works within a frame of reference which does not have to be marked out so long as there is plenty of space for activity within the boundaries which have not yet been drawn. It was by common assumption, rather than by precise definition, that professions acquired authority for activities.

Each kind of work has its own frame of reference, and every time an individual comes for help the professional service which supplies it has implicitly chosen a response within its own framework. Indeed, it may well be the case that while a new approach is being made in one professional service, work within other frames of reference is still being continued in another. Here we may add that we do not see any objection to several workers being involved at one and the same time, as long as each one has some skill in providing something specific that is relevant to a particular individual's needs. Thus, not only is it necessary to have knowledge about what is being done and by whom, but also some knowledge of what it is being done for.

First we must give a list of the frames of reference that we have chosen in order to differentiate some of the different activities with which we are familiar. We shall follow this with a more detailed description of each separate frame.

Moving Towards Uncertainty

Underlying the move from traditional models of working into an exploration of areas of common interest is the move from certainty to uncertainty. In medicine, for example, the work which carries the highest esteem is that based on diagnosis. This medical model of diagnosis, notwithstanding some recent pungent criticisms, has led to advances in medical practice and is utilized in procedures which have improved the general health of the community. Nevertheless, doctors in general, and psychiatrists in particular, have been faced with the problems which cannot be made to fit the medical model (which will be described more fully later). Many clinicians have not hesitated to step out of the area of certainty and enter into areas which are on the fringe of existing knowledge. Paradoxically, workers in other professions have shown a tendency when dealing with problems of human relationships, and with the quality of the provisions for living, to turn towards the traditional medical model. They have attempted to transpose the medical model with its certainties into a system of finding some finality even in those areas in which value systems continue to prevail. The medical model has its questions: What is it? What has caused it? How do we recognize it? How do we treat it? The questions continue to be asked even when they are completely inappropriate. One should not make an illness out of unhappiness, and yet unhappiness should not be ignored.

The diagnostic system is the one from which the remedial professions start. Its inadequacies for some of the experiences of human distress have forced many workers to emerge from this framework. There will always remain an urge to return to it. The pattern of progress seems to be certainty/challenge to the certainty/creative uncertainty, which leads either to toleration of uncertainty as an essential quality or to an attempt to reach new levels of certainty.

The diagnostic system (at its very good best) embodies some of the certainties of observation and inference. Within the diagnostic system there are different dimensions of diagnosis—all of which imply the polarization of normality and abnormality.

What we wish to avoid is a comparable polarization within each successive frame of reference that we shall consider.

In the maturational frame of reference[1] progress is in the form of physical growth. The single fertilized ovum passes through embryonic stages to the event of birth. The extra-uterine life is conventionally

[1] q.v. Chapter 7, Frames of Reference.

represented by the stages of infancy, childhood, adolescence, and adult life, which is followed by degenerative changes and death. Coincidentally, at all stages there are the anomalies of accidents and illnesses. In general, the maturational process is pictured as passing from immaturity to maturity, but these are not the equivalent of abnormality and normality. Every stage has its own criteria, and it is a falsification to idealize a period of adult life as being the norm which one gradually attains and which one eventually loses. At any one point in life there is some change from the previous experience and, even at the latest stages, there is the prospect of some experience that is entirely new. Those who have compassionately studied and assisted people in terminal illness recognize that the dying patient is able to express thoughts and ideas that have never occurred to him before. In the broadest sense, dying (at any age) itself is still conceivable as a stage of development. An understanding of the developmental processes makes it possible to give help that is sometimes necessary when passing through any of the successive stages.

No frame of reference can stand alone. The maturational frame of reference was invoked as one example of the means of escaping from the polarities of normality and abnormality. The diagnostic system still has to be kept in mind where there are anomalies of development, but the process of diagnosis requires the simultaneous employment of notions of the stages that an individual has arrived at on the maturational scale.

The framework of provisions may seem to have its polarities in terms of deprivation and provision. These, too, are not the equivalent of abnormality and normality. It is true that there are provisions which are necessary for the very maintenance of existence, but beyond these there are provisions which have a value that varies in different communities in different circumstances. Provision and deprivation are relative terms. When the term deprivation is used, it is defined in terms of the provisions which, though thought necessary, are lacking.

The next frame of reference is in terms of the relationships between individuals. The life of an infant is a stage in the development of the mother and of the father. Development consists of progressively changing relationships in terms of individuality and interaction. Here again it is tempting to think of relationships as having an essential polarity of normality and abnormality—perhaps isolation being the abnormality and interaction the normality—but arguments will be later marshalled against this idea.

In our attempts to be comprehensive we have to refer (even though it is beyond the scope of our direct professional experience) to the material and non-material circumstances which surround the individual. Matters of finance, housing, the qualities of schools, and the public amenities affect the individual for good or bad.

Individual distress is sometimes discussed in terms of what is thought necessary to provide individual well-being. Sometimes the diagnostic framework is borrowed in making a very necessary recommendation for more adequate housing and at least the minimum spending power. Necessary as these measures may be, the provision is justified within its own frame of reference, and not to "cure" an illness nor to make bad behaviour into good behaviour.

At a higher level of abstraction from the individual there is the politico-socio-economic frame of reference—goodness and badness are equated with systems of administration and of government. There are good and bad systems, and sometimes the systems seem to exist independently of those whose lives depend upon the way that human institutions are organized. It is a worthy aim to attempt to change the system which proves itself to be unsatisfactory. The professional worker, who has authorization in one particular frame of reference, has also an obligation to take a share in the shaping and reshaping of the overall social pattern. This does not detract from obligations to the work in his chosen profession. No one has been given authorization to stand outside the social system and make an objective diagnosis of its normality and abnormality. Even when we can see blatant political wrongs, it is from within a perspective different from that in which professional observations are made.

Some of these frames of reference are outside the limit of the authors of this book. We shall limit ourselves to the following frames of reference: diagnosis, maturation, provision, and relationships. We shall not escape the confusion of making incidental reference to the circumstances of living and some of the politically derived problems of professional organization and administration. The whole purpose of using these frames of reference is to create a structure in which the professional workers in different services can exchange ideas with one another and can co-ordinate their activities and point to gaps in the services that are available.

Practical Implications

We have thought it necessary to give this general outline of the frames of reference that we shall describe in more detail later. But in order to give a touch of reality to a theoretical formulation we should like to tie these ideas down to a clinical example. The one we have selected is a hypothetical case, chosen not by us but by the copywriters of an advertisement for a drug firm. Even if this case were somewhat fictional, we would acknowledge that it represents thousands of real situations. What follows, therefore, in the next chapter will be our personal response to the advertiser's image of how the doctor uses drugs in order to cope with some of the problems of his patients.

5

Focusing on a Practical Problem

SOME years ago a reputable drug firm, advertising in the *British Medical Journal*,[1] displayed a picture of a worried-looking young woman facing a kitchen sink in which there was an untidy pile of unwashed pans and crockery. With one arm she was holding a young baby, and tugging at the other arm was a slightly older child, standing at her side and clamouring for her attention. The text reads:

> The young mother. This poor girl has so many problems. Every time she comes to see you she complains about something else. Her husband is doing badly in his job. She is afraid of another pregnancy. They have a big mortgage to pay off, bills to pay, children to feed, a house to clean. She says she just can't take it any longer.

Below this is the conclusion which is the advertiser's prescription to the doctor. It is remarkable for its simplicity and comprehensiveness. In heavy type it reads:

"She needs the true tranquillizing effect of —."[2]

Multiple Complaints

The complex problems, portrayed in picture and words, have been simplified in the end to a single disorder with a single treatment. The disorder is perceived in medical terms and the treatment is exclusively within the doctor's territorial boundaries.

---

[1] *Br. med. J.*, Vol. 2, 17 September (1966).

[2] There is no reason for the name of the drug to be suppressed. It has an acknowledged range of usefulness which has been established by impeccably conducted clinical studies. Equally, there is no reason in this context to identify the drug.

No doubt it is possible that successful intervention in one area of a complex problem will allow the individual to take command of other disorders which previously were only marginally beyond his or her scope. It can be granted that a tranquillizing drug might benefit such a young mother to the extent that her anxiety level would be reduced to something tolerable. In this particular case, however, each one of the clearly expressed separate complaints clamour as much as the child for separate attention.

Who else should have been involved?

"Her husband is doing badly in his job."

He could get help from a personnel officer, or be referred to an industrial rehabilitation unit or some counselling service. He might even need some physical or mental investigation and treatment on his own account.

"She is afraid of another pregnancy."

She might seek and require contraceptive advice and supplies, or alternatively she might need gynaecological investigation at a hospital. The effects of previous confinements might need surgical treatment. Her general health and level of nutrition might well require a check.

"They have a big mortgage to pay off, bills to pay."

How are they managing their finances on the husband's present wage? Do they need help from Social Security? Are these problems (and some of the preceding ones also) an aspect of unsatisfactory marital interaction? It might be helpful to suggest marriage guidance counselling, casework, or therapy; and who would decide whether the couple should be channelled to a voluntary organization, a social service agency under local authority, or a marital therapy unit within the hospital system?

"Children to feed, a house to clean."

This may be a further indication of the mother's feeling of physical or mental inadequacy; but these aspects, in their own right, are an entitlement to consideration for a home help, which could be mediated through a health visitor who would be concerned with the young children.

"She says she just can't take it any longer."

Who, if anyone, is taking notice of her complaints? It may well be that if she is given a tranquillizer, it will deal with the complaint that she complains!

"Every time she comes to see you she complains about something else."

A sedative will stop her from complaining to the doctor! The tranquillizer may at times be the doctor's answer to the cry for help when he meets with a call which goes beyond the range of his skill and authorization.

However beneficial this drug might or might not have been to the patient in this hypothetical case, there is no doubt that the prescription does a good service to the doctor. It permits him to respond as a doctor to a complex situation of behaviour, or performance, and of attitudes to the values prevalent in the culture which encloses the doctor and the patient. The prescription of the drug would imply that a diagnosis can be made in terms of categories of illness familiar to the doctor. It might almost be said that the diagnosis follows the treatment that is available to the doctor.

Fitting the Diagnosis to the Treatment

Ostensibly the doctor chooses the treatment after he has made the diagnosis, but in this case the prescription of the tranquillizer is a decision made in response to the patient's cry for help. It has been impossible to enclose the totality of the various statements in the advertisement in any single social, psychological, or somatic pathology, and yet a single drug has been prescribed. The question in the doctor's mind would not be, "What is the treatment for this diagnosis?", because he has made no such diagnosis. The question rather is, "What is the diagnosis for this treatment?", and the doctor that has to find words such as "anxiety state" to convey to the patient that the treatment is directed to some disorder which falls into a diagnostic category. If the tranquillizing drug is effective, the woman becomes a patient, suffering from the condition for which this drug should be prescribed. Without the possession of the drug as a means of treatment, the doctor might have had doubts as to whether the woman's complaints were appropriate for the service which he had to offer. The drug brought the manifold complaints into one system, which had one treatment and one diagnosis, capable of being dealt with by one profession.

In discussing the message of the advertisement, line by line, it has been shown that the one-profession, one-treatment formulation of a complex problem can be resolved into a number of components where each component calls for a separate treatment.

There is no justification whatever for assuming that this woman's multiple complaints can be enclosed within a single category of disorder. It was tempting to try to find a single *underlying* primary problem with a variety of symptoms which can then be considered to be secondary; and, in fact, it has been customary within medicine to seek one single pathology for a patient's complaints no matter how numerous and varied they may seem. In traditional medicine the doctor thought he was failing the principles of diagnosis if he ended up with double or multiple pathology. Sometimes a compromise formulation was that the pattern of the one underlying disease had been obscured by "complications".

Alternative Approaches

This woman's complaint might well have reached a social service department as an alternative to a medical practitioner's surgery. She would need to have a presenting complaint in order to enter the door of the department or to bring a social worker to her home. A school teacher may have called attention to some neglect in the care of the older child, or a health visitor might be justifiably anxious about the progress of the infant. Either might initiate intervention of a social service department; the mother herself might have approached a social worker with whom she had had some previous contact, and it would be enough for her just to say she needed help without specifying the nature of her distress. But a social service department also needs some diagnostic formulation, and here also it might be implied that there were a number of presenting social symptoms due to a single underlying disorder—perhaps described as "a disorder of family relationships". Equally, the diagnosis might have been presented in terms of lack of material resources which were necessary but not available to this family. Other specialized services might have been approached. The choice of service does not depend on some essential feature in the problem, but on who complains and to whom.

One would not have to go far back in history for a time when the problem described above would not have been thought of as one which should receive professional help. One would not have to look far even today to find many such problems that neither seek nor receive help. This is not to say that they do not *need* help. It would be fair to say that some of the professional services to which we have briefly referred in the detailed discussion of the advertisement have been created in the image of the kind of worker who would be necessary to provide a particular kind of help.

The woman's visit to the doctor makes it plain that, in her view, the help that she needs goes beyond that which is available within her own family. It is this which makes it necessary for the contribution to be a professional one. Her choice of a doctor as her helper also allows us to infer that she assumes (under the conditions of the National Health Service in Britain) that the help can be provided without charge (or almost without charge, if one takes into account the payment towards the cost of the prescription). The relationship is not simply that between patient and doctor but that between patient, doctor, and community.

Social Role of Medical, Educational, and Welfare Services

Medical treatment is part of the social services in a broad sense, and these include education, various material welfare services, and what have recently been called the "personal social services" which are part of the responsibility of social service departments.

The rapid growth of social services is particularly a feature of industrialized societies with a rising standard of living. It appears that the organized community, which imposes obligations and gives entitlements to the individuals who comprise that community, finds it intolerable to contemplate excessive divergencies in health, in material provision, or in levels of performance. The social services in general were created to give a minimum standard to those who could not achieve this themselves. Gradually they have come to be used by all classes, either during temporary vicissitudes or to increase the level of standard of living which they have achieved for themselves. Even the affluent do not hesitate to use the child's allowance, or the nursery or playgroup facilities, and to shop around where possible for some of the ancillary provisions of education and other statutory services.

The growth of the social services has been gradual, and provision for needs is unequally distributed geographically, and is far from complete. The aims are comprehensive, but the achievement depends upon the development of separate skills backed by resources supported by local initiative.

Social work now appears to be following a pattern of progress similar to that pursued in the past by medicine.

Social work came into existence in a number of separate fields in which other professions took the lead. Social work came into existence to make up for deficiencies of communication of specialists with fields of their own. The social worker was expected to be an expert in communication, but the theme of the communication was related to a specialism created by someone else. More recently social workers from these different fields gathered themselves together to develop a theory and practice of their own, and have built up a generic training which is intended to equip a social worker for social work in any one of these fields. Social service departments were founded on the principle that a social worker could be a generalist and the problems that arose in special situations (be they medical, educational, or those dealing with the material environment) would respond to an analysis of an underlying social and personal disorder. Experience has now been gained of the limitations of a general approach, and a search for some valid specialist boundaries, not necessarily the old divisions, has begun, indicating a recognition that the presentation of problems in different situations is an essential part of the problem itself.

Every profession either claims or is given its boundaries. The professional skills are related to the tasks which have to be undertaken. But tasks which are related to human problems seem to refuse to be confined by arbitrarily drawn boundary lines. Professions have the double problem of sometimes feeling unwilling or unable to carry out unexpected tasks while, at the same time, developing a lively curiosity about problems beyond the territory originally assigned.

Social work, while filling gaps left by other services, has to develop its own traditions and make its own selections of appropriate tasks, even if only to make it possible for social workers to feel secure in their identity. While social work is searching for its proper ethic, it is following the same course as that part of psychiatry which ventured out of the clinical setting of medicine into areas where health and illness are not clearly divisible.

The psychiatrist is envisaged primarily as an expert in the diagnosis and treatment of mental illness, and psychiatry is thus a specialism within medicine. The psychiatrist, however, is called upon (sometimes as an alternative to others who might be called upon) to deal with problems of the upbringing of children, of education, of behaviour, and with the problems of family disharmony, of the sexual activities which go outside some present norm. Sometimes he is called upon to be a specialist in other people's specialities. In common with the present-day social worker he finds that the call for his help is not wholehearted. He may be expected to succeed in producing a result which is demanded by others, but which he himself would not seek. One solution to these ambiguous calls is to make the boundaries clear and to decide on the range of problems which would be excluded.

Professions may work amicably together, each carrying out separate tasks, but in agreement with one another. They may work in competition, either by intruding in one another's work, or alternatively by one profession's trying to foist a difficult problem onto members of another profession. Interdisciplinary work, where a number of professions join together on a common problem, depends upon each one possessing doubts as to its own competence to comprehend the whole. The area of interdisciplinary work is the area into which all the professions are advancing simultaneously. This theme includes a special warning to psychiatrists, who are accustomed to being called in consultation by a variety of other services. It may be possible in some cases to isolate some psychiatric factor which can be dealt with as a clinical psychiatric task.

If we return to the young mother in the advertisement, the prescription of the drug turns the problem exclusively into a remedial one, where the cry for help is an indication of an identifiable disorder and where the drug is its cure. If this were all, the doctor would have been deaf to some of the messages in the patient's cry. But many doctors who prescribe a drug may still show awareness of another part of the message and are able to show that they have understood it. In this case the contribution is the communication to the patient that she need not hide her distress, and that the doctor does not expect the drug to stop her from complaining about the reality of the circumstances which she describes. He may go further and guide her to specialist services which give another kind of help. In this aspect the doctor is an intermediary and not a prescriber, because the other specialist services have the right to make their own appraisal and to decide upon the response they will make. At the same time, the doctor continues to understand the part played by her so-called symptoms in her personal and family life. He has not just passed over the problems as being no concern of his when the responsibility is transferred to someone else. He has given an interpretation of the problems by his actions and his interest.

The Right to Complain

This interpretative function of the doctor is of major importance. It emphasizes the severity of the impact of the external conditions on the individual. Conventional formulations are in some way derogatory of the individual who fails to cope. The implication is that she should have been able to put up with the conditions, but if she is not doing so, she has the excuse that the conditions are making her ill. The illness can be treated, the conditions cannot! There is no getting away from the frequent implication that a person who breaks down under these conditions is of weaker moral fibre, and the purpose of the treatment is to enable her to get better and put up with the conditions, as other people do!

The approach to the doctor may well be preferred to the cry of despair which is directed to a social service department to come to the aid of a social casualty; and somewhere it is necessary to offer the interpretation that it is an assault on human dignity to assume that anyone who cannot cope with personal, family, and social obligations must be labelled either inadequate or ill.

A more recent advertisement of the same genre illustrates the point further.

The main picture is of a tower block. An inset shows a woman, once again at the kitchen sink, interrupting the drying of a plate in order to hold one hand to her forehead. The gesture is a dramatic representation of her vain attempt to "get a grip on herself". The main caption is:

> ... loneliness and despair halfway to the sky.

The reading matter below states:

> The depression which can follow an adverse change in circumstances, such as living in a high-rise flat, is usually of the neurotic or reactive kind. These types of depression usually respond best to therapy with ...

The advertisement goes on to quote from psychiatric papers which link the word "anxiety" with "depressive disorders of the neurotic kind". This provides the cue for the statement that the particular drug relieves anxiety and that it is recommended for "comprehensive treatment of depression or anxiety".

It is impossible to criticize the use of the drug which is being advertised, or even to criticize the content of the advertisement, without putting oneself at a disadvantage. The woman whose photograph is captured on the advertisement page is indeed a captive in her high-level flat. She may not have any other choice. Why should she not have the benefit of a tranquillizing drug? But where is there any indication that her so-called "symptoms" are, in fact, a *normal* reaction to these conditions?

Is it not in some ways an insult to her to suggest that her despair can be soothed by drugs? If the best answer is for her to move away from these flats, it could be said that the next best thing would be to smother her feelings with tranquillizing drugs. But what would become of any anger she might feel towards the remote planners who designed the flats, the committees which approved the project, and the officials who were unable to give her any alternative? Is she not also entitled to feel anger towards her husband (not portrayed in the advertisement), who may be unable to comprehend her difficulty because he himself, being out at work all day, does not experience it? And could she not also have a feeling of anger towards the doctor who answers her complaint with a prescription which is expected to put things right?

But if the woman is trapped, so is the doctor, because he has been trained to see problems as symptoms, to see symptoms as a step towards diagnosis, and diagnosis as a prerequisite to treatment.

Vulnerability

The doctor may escape by widening the concept of diagnosis to include conditions which are outside the traditional medical framework. If he does so, he leaves his medical authority behind him. His prescription in the social field will not necessarily be dispensed, and he is subject to the same frustrations and delays in the carrying out of his perfectly sensible recommendations as is, say, the social worker or, for that matter, the ordinary member of the public.

Considerable pressure is exerted on the doctor to look upon words which are descriptive of feelings as being the equivalent of symptoms of clinical conditions. In the two drug advertisements used as illustrations, the words "anxiety" and "depression" have been seized upon, and a clinical structure has been built on the foundation of those descriptive words. An interesting feature of this is that in the image of diseases created in this fashion women by far outnumber men—at least, if we go by the evidence of the illustrations in the advertisements. Fashions change, however, with prevailing conditions. An even more recent advertisement gives an illustration of a man sitting face to face with his doctor, exhibiting an agonizing expression. Here, the main caption reads:

The anxiety of redundancy can be depressing.

The text underneath the picture begins:

> For the middle-aged male, redundancy and subsequent interviews for re-employment can constitute stress situations evoking anxiety and depression.

People are inclined to turn to drugs for relief from some of the hazards of living, and once again it is necessary to state that no one should be denied any relief which is effective. And yet the role of "patient" seems inappropriate in these circumstances. Psychotherapy can be subject to the same reservations as the use of drugs. One of Karl Jasper's wise sayings was that one should not seek in psychotherapy what life should give.[3]

[3] JASPERS, KARL, *The Nature of Psychotherapy*, Manchester University Press, 1963.

The words "anxiety" and "depression" may refer in some circumstances to the most normal response possible to situations which are an inescapable part of life. There can be too much, too little, or the appropriate amount of anxiety or depression. When one turns too rapidly to a therapeutic process, it is a debasement both of the human experience and of the methods used to treat the abnormalities which differ qualitatively or quantitatively from what one might ordinarily encounter.

F. J. Croockshank, writing 60 years ago on the disbelief of surgeons in the psychogenesis of ulcerative colitis, referred to the alterations in the functions of the bladder and bowel with variations in emotional states. He said that he confidently expected to see learned papers on a condition called "paroxysmal lachrymation". The treatment would be a salt-free diet and a restriction of fluids, and limitation of tobacco, alcohol, and sexual excess; if those failed, recourse would have to be made to surgical excision of the lachrymal glands! He did not live to see the name "paroxysmal nocturnal polyruia" given, in all seriousness, to bed-wetting.[4]

The final message of this chapter is that there is no need to translate every "cry for help" into some technical jargon which implies a diagnosis of an underlying disorder. In many cases the response to a cry for help should be *help*. There are cases when to apply a technical term is a way of avoiding help, and we still remain with the problem of recognizing the authority and competence to give the help which in fact we offer.

---

[4] CROOCKSHANK, F.J. Organ jargon, *Br. J. med. Psychol.* **10** (4), 295–311 (1930).

6
Dimensions of Diagnosis

MODERN medicine, which prides itself on being scientific, is based on the diagnosis of disease. Before a diagnosis can be made there is an underlying assumption that diseases are separate from health and that each disease is separable from other diseases.

In the early stages of medical history it frequently was enough to give a name to the symptom which was complained of. The observations of the physician were called "signs". Regularly occurring patterns of symptoms and signs became designated "syndromes". The next development was to link symptoms and signs with alterations in the chemical and physical state of the body (the "pathology"). When causal agents were identified (the "aetiology") the pattern was complete, and the notion of disease had achieved definition.

A disease was thus recognized by its symptoms, signs, pathology, and aetiology. The pathology became the rational basis of treatment, the aetiology the basis of prevention.

The number of ways in which a person can be ill has multiplied along with the progress in organizing observations about the illness. There has, therefore, been a demand for the classification of categories of disease. The idea developed that the disease is a concrete entity with an existence of its own, independent of the person who is diseased. People go on to speak of "the natural history of disease" and presumably they are referring to what happens with a disease which is uncomplicated by attempts to treat it.

The idea of a disease entity is a convenient fiction. The saying goes, translated from the French, "There are no illnesses, only ill people."

The fiction of the disease entity has, however, been one of the most valuable concepts in the study and treatment of ill people. The diagnosis allows the disease to be given a name under which observations can be recorded and communicated. Medicine fits scientific principles most nearly when observations can be made in a form where one worker's results can be compared with those of others. It may be convenient to forget that diseases are notional and that they have no existence except as a way of conceptualizing the experience of the patient and the observations of those who come to his aid. Linnaeus, who created a classification of plants, which have an objective reality, went on to invent a classification of diseases, which are concepts. He stated convincingly, "Names are the first letters of all knowledge ... because without them nothing can be learned."

The Magic of Naming

The process of naming a disease has a value in itself. Once something is named, it is felt to be under control. This is the magic of naming. Doctors and patients alike feel more comfortable when the disease is named, even if it is an incurable one. Otherwise they still bear a responsibility for further investigations. Frequently it is enough to turn the English word for a symptom or complaint into Latin or Greek. There are very many reasons why a schoolchild may find difficulty in reading. Each explanation should have a different consequence. But if "difficulty with words" is translated into Greek, the label "dyslexia" is taken to be a diagnosis. It is implied that such a diagnosis requires no other explanation, and it is assumed that the diagnosis represents a specific condition for which a standardized treatment can be devised. This type of thinking follows inevitably from using a descriptive label as if it were a diagnosis. How can anyone resist the conclusion that "dyslexia" means more than "difficulty with words"?

The use of such a descriptive word is a short cut to a diagnosis that may exclude relevant information about the individual child, the family relationships, and the previous educational experience. In choosing the example of dyslexia as a description, rather than as a diagnosis, we are allowing ourselves to enter an area of challenge and controversy, and we are asking for trouble! Emotions are readily aroused amongst parents, teachers, neurologists, psychologists, and psychiatrists as to whether or not such a condition as dyslexia exists. One thing is certain. When the word is used as a diagnosis, it is expected that some special educational provision will be found for the child. The name thus has power for good so long as the benefits are not looked upon as being so presently available as to give cause for complaint if they are not realized.

In general medicine there are many instances where there is abundant confidence in the goodness and efficacy of what the doctor has to offer. A patient who is bleeding from an internal organ has been known to gain reassurance from the fact that the doctor uses a technical term such as "haematemesis" or even just "haemorrhage". These words also serve, for the time being, as a diagnosis in the period before a comprehensive and precise diagnosis is made. This is as it should be, because the further investigations are accompanied by the treatment which is appropriate to the state of emergency.

Naming is not always a comfort. The magic sometimes carries fears. A general practitioner had to arrange for the examination of the sputum of a girl suspected of having tuberculosis. He visited the home to bring the report of the examination. The girl's mother looked at his face and said, "Don't say it, doctor." It was if the condition did not exist until the ominous name had been disclosed.[1]

At another level, naming has a value in calling attention to the contemporary advances in professional practice. This applies even when the name itself is not entirely appropriate or satisfactory. Without the name "battered baby syndrome" many cases would not be recognized. It is the name which has allowed doctors, nurses, and members of the general public to take notice of something which has always existed, but which was not observed because it could scarcely be believed. How could it be noticed if it had no name? And how could a name be given if doctors, nurses, and social workers at a hospital accepted the parents' explanation for the child's injuries? After a name had been given it was possible to recognize that plausible explanations given by parents would not stand up to closer examination. Nevertheless, there is something unsatisfactory about using the term

---

[1] This was in the days before chemotherapy radically changed the prognosis of pulmonary tuberculosis for the better.

"syndrome" for a situation in which there are many participants. The term is insufficient to describe the injuries to the child and the complex personality features and interactions of the parents. The multi-faceted situation can only be dealt with by entering simultaneously, or consecutively, into separate frames of reference. The child's needs for safety may be in conflict with the parents' need for confirmation of the ability to be a parent. The use of the name of the "syndrome" is not an authorization for any one profession to take charge. The doctor, the health visitor, the social worker, the teacher, and the representatives of the law have different criteria for their activity; but there are some decisions which can only be taken by agreement with them all.

Determining the Treatment

Within traditional medicine, and when dealing with what is described as a disease entity (which is somehow enclosed with the personality of an individual patient) the diagnosis provided criteria for prescribing treatment. Occasionally, the relationship between treatment and diseases is so precise that the response to treatment could be a feature of the diagnosis. A further characteristic of the diagnosis is its relationship to prognosis or outcome. The concept of prognosis is the accumulation of experience of the results of treatment. Some diseases are characterized by an unvaryingly bad outcome, and many would instance schizophrenia as an example. It becomes a matter of faith with some that any patient so diagnosed who unexpectedly recovers must have been mistakenly diagnosed!

The treatment of mental illness poses problems that go beyond those of understanding and treating physical illness. Most mental illnesses with regularly occurring patterns of disturbed thought, feelings, behaviour, and relationships have no identifiable physical pathology. The disorder enters into every aspect of the patient's living.

A child with some mental or emotional disorder has his life in the school, the family, and the neighbourhood; the adult has a role in the family, at work, and in the community. Obviously, professional people other than doctors are involved in their own right and not under any other professional direction.

What applies to mental illness applies also to chronic disability from any cause, hereditary or acquired. The doctor is expected to play his part, but there are many aspects of the patient's disabilities of which the doctor has no knowledge and for which he cannot, or should not, prescribe.

Within classically taught clinical medicine, there are five categories of disease which can be enumerated on the thumb and four fingers of one hand. The first category is hereditary disease; the other four are acquired: injuries, inflammation or infections, degenerations, and new growths. This system completely leaves out deficiency diseases (unless they could be accommodated under degenerations), any mental illness in which there is no organic change, and all problems of behaviour and of interpersonal relationships. These are the areas in which traditional medical diagnostic concepts are insufficient, and these are areas also in which other professions often have as clear a responsibility as do the medical services. Whatever the theoretical or philosophical basis, doctors in general will continue to be consulted about these problems.

An attempt has been made to keep some of these problems within the medical framework by the creation of terms such as social medicine and community medicine, which give the medical person the authorization to share with other professions in the study and treatment of problems that cannot be conceptualized as being within single individuals. For these problems the doctor must at times abandon the diagnostic frame of reference and find an appropriate place within one or more of the frames of reference that are shared by other professions.

Notions of Disease

Even within the diagnostic framework, and within the field of traditional medicine, some adaptations have to be made to the concept of the specific disease entity. Within medicine itself there are different dimensions of diagnosis, and some of these dimensions can be put to good use by members of other professions.

Cohen,[2] writing on "The Evolution of the Concept of Disease", traced the history of rational medicine through the various Greek schools down to the medicine of the last three centuries, and found two main concepts that

---

[2] COHEN, H., The evolution of the concept of disease, *Proc. R. Soc. Med.* **48**, 155 (1955).

have dominated all writing on the nature of disease. The first was of disease as a distinct entity. The second concept was described as a deviation from the normal. In the deviation Cohen gives a complex formula to refer to the large number of separate factors which bring about varying degrees of departure (physically and mentally) from the normal. In the disease, a healthy man A falls ill and becomes $A + B$, where B is the disease.

We shall accept this formulation, but we shall elaborate the category of deviation and add to it the idea of dysfunction.

Diseases (Disease Entities)

These are best represented by acute illness, physical or mental, that can conveniently be considered as separate from the idealized "normality" of the healthy personality. A disease is a specific entity. With illnesses such as pneumonia or appendicitis it is possible to say whether the illness is present or not present. The responsibility for treatment is entirely medical or surgical. If a man has pneumonia it does not matter whether he is a good husband or a bad husband, a good father or a bad father, a good workman/colleague/employer or a bad one. All other activities are in suspense and the treatment takes priority. Everything concerned with the patient is under the orders of the doctor, whose authority derives from the fact that he is dealing with matters of life and death.

The authority of the doctor spreads to the treatment of illnesses that are less serious and less acute, but many illnesses, even of a specific nature, may conveniently be considered under other dimensions of diagnosis at some stage in the course of the illness.

A few mental illnesses may be regarded under the dimension of disease entities, at least during some of their stages.

When illness is perceived in the dimension of a specific disease entity the aim is to cure. When the individual A has had added to him the disease B, treatment removes B and leaves A as he was before. The illness is thus an episode in the life of an otherwise normal individual.

Illness does not always follow this idealized pattern: a cure is not always obtainable, and we cannot always assume a previously healthy state. Moreover, there are many illnesses of long duration where a partial disability remains. For this reason, and for many others, we must consider alternative dimensions of diagnosis.

Cohen's second concept could include two different formulations, i.e. (a) disordered function, and (b) deviation that is distinguished from the normal, not by a multiplicity of specific factors, but by the *degree* of departure from a statistical norm. We would then have three separate dimensions of diagnostic concepts:

> *Diseases* (discussed above)
> *Dysfunctions*
> *Deviations.*

To these one might add one further dimension *Descriptions* (already mentioned), to enclose the diagnosis, which is merely a technical term that adds nothing to the information given by the patient.

Dysfunctions

Here the important question is not whether a person *has* an illness or not, but refers to the functions in which he is adversely affected. The treatment is aimed not directly at the disease (even if a specific disease can be identified), but towards developing some capacity or performance which is absent or impaired. In this sense treatment is directed not to the pathology but to a normal part of the personality.

Within this dimension it is possible to take into account a large number of factors which include inherited constitution, previous provision and deprivation, beneficial and harmful experiences, and the immediate circumstances connected with the onset of the disorder. The disability of chronic illness can be considered in this manner, and it is immediately apparent that the person's normal and abnormal activities affect a large number of other people who may have some responsibility for the treatment.

When thinking of illness as a disorder of function one must consider the person's assets and potentialities, as well as disabilities and defects, and take into account the way that the person receives, or is denied, support from other people. The illness may be studied from the point of view of individual personality, environmental background, or interpersonal relationships. Treatment or intervention may be primarily channelled into any one of these three areas or into any combination of them.[3]

Within this dimension we could include the failure to acquire the expected control of bladder and bowel, some of the failures of learning at school, and some of the consequential disabilities of previous physical or mental disorders. The aetiological factors are complex: the symptoms are represented by changes in the way a person performs and experiences his various activities. Treatment has to enter into the different functional fields, and the doctor's responsibility is shared with others.

The word "treatment" is not a medical monopoly and there are experts with skills related to particular functions. We have occupational therapy, physiotherapy, psychotherapy, remedial reading, in all of which a separate professional training exists. The individual who is a patient, receiving medical treatment, is also the concern of members of other professions who deal with the whole range of population. The treatment does not remove the obligations and entitlements to education, to housing, and to financial support when eligible. Nor does the term automatically absolve the patient from legal responsibilities for his conduct.

The different professional services may be involved simultaneously or in sequence. Different professions may have to take the lead during different phases of the illness or disability. At some stages the professional services are required to work in co-operation with one another and, on occasion, one service is called upon to take a predominating part. The use of the dimension of dysfunction allows one to consider the idea of a multi-disciplinary team. Thus, the expression of the illness is multi-dimensional, the causation multi-factorial, and the treatment multi-disciplinary.[4]

Deviations

In this dimension one does not ask what a person has, or in what way his functioning is disordered. Instead one asks how much, or how little,

---

[3] KAHN, J. H. and WRIGHT, S. E., *Human Growth and Development*, 3rd edn., Pergamon Press, London, 1980.

[4] KAHN, J. H., *Case Conference*, **13** (March), 385 (1967).

a person is expressing or experiencing a quality which exists in every individual—normal or otherwise. The deviation is from either a statistical norm or an ideal one. The concept of deviation applies particularly to so-called "*behaviour disorders*" which are relative to the culture. It also applies to the experience of *emotional* distress and *well-being*. There are instances where *physical conditions* of the body are adjudged normal or abnormal by standards which are far from absolute.

The use of the term "disorder", as in "behaviour disorder", is the enemy of clear thinking. There is a hidden implication that the disorder is a disease entity which has its form of expression, its recognizable signs, its internal characteristics, and its recognized treatment and possible preventative measures. The implication is that, like disease, it has symptoms, signs, aetiology, and pathology. It must be emphasized that deviation is a departure from standards which are a product of the culture and the criteria are inevitably subjective. There could be no call for intervention unless the values of goodness and badness are applied. A behaviour disorder is behaviour which is disapproved. In some cases the behaviour can be judged by religious criteria and referred to as "*sinful*". If legal standards are applied to the same behaviour it is termed "*delinquency*". If it becomes termed "*behaviour disorder*" in a diagnostic framework the implication is that the behaviour is *illness*. The choice of the context determines the consequence. Sinfulness requires expiation, reparation, or absolution. Delinquency implies the processes of law with its punitive, retributive, and deterrant intentions. Illness implies treatment and a freedom from personal responsibility for the behaviour.

It has already been indicated that the concept of behaviour disorder is relative to the culture. Behaviour is judged as normal or abnormal according to geographical area. What is normal in one country may be abnormal in another; within one country the standards vary from town to town and even in different districts of the same town. There are variations according to social class factors, religion, prevailing occupation, ethnic origin, and the transmigration of people bringing standards from other countries. There is the problem of migrants who preserve in their country of adoption a culture which has already been abandoned in their country of origin. There are even the problems of standards applied to children by parents who are half a generation older than the parents of the child's schoolmates. There are problems of criteria which are applied differentially to children in their homes, neighbourhood, and schools. Some children share a culture with their family and their neighbours while remaining hostile to the culture of school—and are therefore called deviant. There are some cases where the home shares a culture with the school in opposition to the neighbourhood. Some children can adapt to two kinds of lives but not to three. In any case, it is inappropriate to consider the deviation as the equivalent of a disease (when judged by any of these criteria) which requires treatment. This does not imply that the deviation does not create a problem for some person or persons. Moreover, the above considerations should not lead to the conclusion that the psychiatrist, the teacher, and the social worker have nothing to offer when behaviour is perceived as a problem. There are instances when a person's behaviour causes distress directly to the person concerned. Here at least the term disorder can appropriately be applied—the disorder being within conflicting aspects of personality. Treatment eventually allows the individual to take responsibility for changing the behaviour. In this case the behaviour has been perceived and responded to as a cry for help.

In other cases the conflict is interpersonal and affects the whole family; sometimes a larger group or whole culture is implicated. We have still to take into account the instances when the standard by which behaviour is judged has legal authority. The intervention is in the direction of inducing conformity, and a professional service is given the task of imposing constraints. Amongst the critics of psychiatry and social work there are those who object to a professional service becoming the tool of the law. The idea is extended to the imputation that these services do *nothing but* apply social constraints. The cure of mental illness is thought to be an intrusion on the personality of someone who has escaped from the confines of the surrounding culture. There are certainly many instances where normality and abnormality, applied to mental life, owe their origin to what is popularly or conventionally acceptable. There are other instances where the state protects its political system by labelling dissidents as mentally ill. But these very real issues should not cloud the fact that the general range of mental illness leads to behaviour which can be distressing to the person concerned as well as to the family and immediate neighbourhood.

Even when working within legal criteria, the standards are never permanent. Delinquency can only be defined as being what the law says it is—the law has to work within its own definitions as enacted by the legislature. The laws change, sometimes by the force of public opinion and sometimes in advance of it. The professional worker shares in and sometimes leads the formation of public opinion. He uses the personal part of his personality and draws on informed professional experience.

The three dimensions of diagnosis have their implications for treatment.

Diseases are cured (hopefully), and the professional service is medical. Other professions bring in their skills within the medical orbit.

Dysfunctions may be treated by one or more of a number of professions; each bodily function may be the main study of some particular medical or non-medical speciality. Interdisciplinary work, team work, may recognize the complementary skills, but someone seeking help may come fortuitously to one professional service rather than to another. Medical, social work, and teaching professions have areas of both separate and common concern, and choice may be a matter of chance.

In *deviations* the criteria may be mainly social, and the aim is to produce conformity. It may also be a valid professional service to challenge the criteria of disorder and to enlarge the tolerance of the community in general. In many cases the professional task is to enlarge the tolerance of the individual concerned to his *own* behaviour and experiences. It may not be easy to do this if the person himself has interpreted his unwelcome behaviour as being sinful or criminal, and this is an example of the need to redefine the initial presentation in order to allow treatment.

Descriptions

Mention has already been made of Descriptions as a dimension of diagnosis which makes no professional contribution to its understanding. Dyslexia and the battered baby syndrome are examples. So is "hyperkinesia", which means no more than "over-activity". The danger of these descriptive labels is that they may be used to justify a standardized treatment. A child may be described as "over-active" when living in an upper floor of high-rise flats. It is impossible for the mother to allow the child to play alone at ground level, but the child's *normal* activities within the home wear out the mother's tolerance. Similarly, the child's normal activities may be disapproved of when living in rooms in the house of relatives, or in the house of a landlord who wants to evict his sub-tenants. Such children's behaviour gradually becomes abnormal by anyone's standards. Yet if the over-activity is labelled "hyperkinesia", it is then implied that it is an abnormality in the child for which some physical treatment is necessary.

The criticism in the foregoing pages of the use of descriptive terms as if they were diagnoses is a semantic one, but nonetheless, it has far-reaching practical consequences. The names that people use as diagnoses affect their actions. There is an extensive literature about "Learning Disorders in Children". The word "disorder" in the title begs the question of the location of the problem.

In a recent American publication[5] it was stated, "Learning disabilities represent the largest single class of medical problems of American children today." It is assumed that the disorder is "neurogenic" and the editor adds, "This difficulty seems to affect between 5% and 20% of the non-retarded child population, depending upon how learning disabilities are defined." No indication is given of the nature of the relevant neurological factors, but the diagnoses seem to be supported by descriptions of the children's behaviour, which was "driving the mother clean out of her skull". The most appalling feature is the recommendation of drug treatment for these conditions, using amphetamine chlorpromazine. This could well become the modern equivalent of the reputed Victorian practice of giving gin or laudanum to restless children.

So far the use of the term "hyperactivity" as a diagnosis has been on a much smaller scale in this country than in the U.S.A., but the numbers so diagnosed are beginning to increase. A sociologist, Steven Box,[6] comments on the disturbing fact that as there is no valid physical sign of such a disease, the diagnosis is made by an evaluation of the child's

---

[5] CANTWELL, D. P. (ed.), *The Hyperactive Child*, Spectrum Publications Inc., New York, 1975.

[6] *New Society*, 1 December, 1977.

behaviour. A questionnaire to be filled by teachers relies upon items such as fidgets, is restless, is inattentive, exhibits behaviour which disturbs other children, is quarrelsome, exhibits destructive behaviour, steals, loses temper.

These complaints, disturbing as they may be to teachers and parents, should have no place as criteria of a condition which is conceptualized as a disease within the child.

The reckless use of diagnostic terms implying neuropathology for overactive children has done a disservice to the recognition of the importance of actual trauma in the perinatal period. A child population study in Newcastle upon Tyne[7] studied two adverse perinatal factors: abnormal delivery (which is potentially modifiable by the obstetrician) and anoxia (which is potentially modifiable by the neonatal practitioner). The numbers were small and the consequences severe: adverse factors occurred in 1% of the population studied. Some comfort is to be obtained from the fact that the great majority turn out to be free of any handicap. Emphasis, however, was placed on breech delivery, prematurity, and low birth weight, which involved the possibility of infant death or of survival with irreversible brain damage. The results included combinations of mental defect, cerebral palsy, and convulsions.

When the consequences of proven brain damage are so severe, it seems to be an outrage to apply the term "brain damage" or "minimal brain damage" on no more evidence than overactivity or low educational performance.

The dimension of specific disease tends to dominate all others, and, whatever the phenomenon (whether some constitutional anomaly, some defects of functioning, or some deviation from a notional norm, or if what is complained of is a social situation), people continue to ask, "What is it?", "What causes it?", and "How do we treat it?".

Emerging from the Diagnostic Framework

The dimensions of dysfunctioning and deviation, which permit one to widen the concepts of diagnosis, also provide a means of emerging

---

[7] NELIGAN, G. *et al.*, *The Formative Years*, Oxford University Press, 1974.

from the diagnostic framework into the other frames of reference. Such, however, is the dominance of the diagnostic framework that many other types of label are given a separate place, as a category of diagnosis, even though they would more appropriately fit into one of the dimensions already discussed or, alternatively, fit more appropriately into entirely different frames of references, yet to be described.

Here are a few examples:

DEFECTIVENESS
DEPRIVATION
DRUG DEPENDENCY
DISORDERS

Even the word "difficulties" has been elevated to the status of a diagnosis; and psychiatric reports sometimes end with the sentence, "This patient is suffering from "difficulties' at school/work/home." The use of the words "suffering from" naturally follows from the use of the diagnostic framework; the absurdity is revealed when a psychiatrist inadvertently concludes his report with a statement, "This child is suffering from a behaviour disorder", when it is other people who suffer.

Defectiveness, for which the word "handicap" is often preferred, can be physical, sensory, or intellectual. When dealing with the cause of the defect we must enter into the dimension of disease entities. When dealing with the performance that is possible we are taken into the dimension of dysfunction. When making comparisons with others in the same age range we enter the dimension of deviation.

Where there is confusion about definitions or the dimension in which a problem is conceptualized, there is, we find, conflict between professions. There is currently some propaganda to remove the whole subject of mental defectiveness from medical services. In one instance it suggests that the care of mentally handicapped children should be transferred to the ordinary educational system. In other cases (this applies particularly to residential care and occupational training) it is the social service departments which either claim or are given responsibility. The medical contribution is expected to provide a once-and-for-all diagnosis, and the treatment to be given is to be either an educational or a social provision. Countering this trend there have been recommendations for continuous assessment and joint care, and these have been given some confirmation in the Court report[8] with its consequential departmental circular.[9]

It is no longer possible to remain within these dimensions of diagnosis and take cognisance of the multitudinous factors which affect the problem being dealt with. So much knowledge has accumulated about human activities that it is necessary, for many purposes, to go beyond the whole system of diagnostic formulations. Professional work utilizes the knowledge which is currently available, and also embodies general hearsay and popular lore which still pervade the thinking of workers in every profession.

The system of diagnostic formulations is never quite adequate in itself to cope with the impact of problems in the helper and the helped, and it has become our task to find further frames of reference for disciplined thinking and for practical applications of professional work.

---

[8] *Fit for the Future*—Report of the Committee on Child Health Services, HMSO, London, December 1976.

[9] Health Circular HC/78/5, Local Authority Circular LAC(78)2, Health Services Development, January 1978.

7

Frames of Reference

THE diagnostic frame of reference discussed in the previous chapter was advanced in the hope that treatment can be selected to fit the different categories of disorder. It is assumed that abnormality can be distinguished from normality, and that there are separate varieties of abnormality. The diagnostic labelling is a step towards finding the appropriate treatment.

Overcoming the Stigma of Labels

This formulation does not do full justice to the ways of treating human problems. The labels of some disorders are associated with stigma in that the label is felt to be a bigger disadvantage than the situation or problem which leads to the labelling. Some progress has been made towards meeting these disadvantages by adding the new dimension of dysfunctions and deviations to specific disease entities. This, however, may not be enough to meet the problem of finding a framework in which to enclose the treatment in cases where distress is connected with:

(a) interaction with others who are participants,
(b) stages of individual development, and
(c) the absence of necessary supplies required to maintain life at the different stages of development.

The kind of treatment will depend upon emphasis on these different ways in which problems can be perceived. Is something felt to be wrong? Where is the abnormality located—in the person, in the close family relationship, in material factors, in the structure and functioning of society, or in the nature of humanity and the universe in which life exists?

Choosing the Frame of Reference

A variety of frames of reference has to be brought into existence in order to make it possible to decide on what action, if any, should be taken when complaints are made. It is little use choosing a framework where the scale is so large that any possible action can have only a minimal effect. But a particular frame may, indeed, be selected for the very purpose of justifying a particular kind of action or, for that matter, no action. It is, of course, a kind of diagnosis to select a framework; but the individual diagnosis is left behind when one focuses on the interaction, the stages of development, the provisions available, or the environmental background of the participants in the problem.

Polarities

The frames of reference (each with its own polarities) to which we shall give particular attention are those in which remedial work of different kinds can be conceptualized in terms of polarities.

Diagnostic	:	Normality/Abnormality
Relationships	:	Isolation/Interaction
Growth	:	Maturity/Immaturity
Supplies	:	Provision/Deprivation

The diagnostic frame of reference, as has already been stated, depends upon the opposition of normality and abnormaltiy. Other frames of reference have their polarities, but it would be misleading to think of these as being the equivalent of the normal and abnormal of the diagnostic system. We shall show later that the substitution of words with different shades of meaning for the words isolation or interaction (for example) put these polarities at different points on the scale of approval/disapproval.

There remain other frames of reference—social, political, and economic—within which it is possible to study the background in which distress is experienced and where help may be provided. There is also the religious frame of reference in which human beings seek meanings of existence and ideas of purpose in the universe. In all the frames of reference it is possible to attach values—good and bad—to the experiences of illness and health. In all of them the attribution is easily reversed, even in cases of illness when it is looked upon as a test of virtue, or as a means of acquiring, through suffering, a higher level of maturity.

Environmental Framework

It is not possible for us here to enumerate all the ways in which external circumstances within the environmental framework affect the individual, or the ways in which the individual, as part of a greater humanity, affects the environment.

The professional worker should take part in calling attention to the ideological, spiritual and material background as professionals in our field as well as in our personal commitment to the community. We also need to join with the so-called "ecologists" in an attempt to preserve natural resources for future generations.

The professional services have their theory and their standards which are to be referred to in the various working frames of reference. There are also the administrative framework in which all the activities are organized; the statutory framework which permits, and sometimes compels, the professional worker's task (the same statutory framework provides the rules for the population as a whole); and the political/social/economic framework, which, although beyond the scope of this book, must be referred to from time to time.

Diagnostic Framework: Preparing for the Social Viewpoint

The diagnostic frame, which has been dealt with more fully in Chapter 6, was originally constructed on the basis of specific disease entities. The new dimensions of dysfunctions and deviations allowed treatment to be extended to the normal part of the individual and then made it possible to challenge the standards by which abnormality had been judged. The progress from diseases to dysfunctions and deviations marked a decreasing medical domination of the field of diagnosis and treatment. By the time that the dimension of deviation is reached a good deal of the discourse remains within the social system in which disorders are perceived and in which remedies are sought.

Relationships: Family and Social Groups

The use of this framework takes us from the individual to family and social groupings. Isolation is opposed to interaction, but this does not imply that isolation is abnormal, nor that interaction is normal. When the words "interaction" and "isolation" are changed slightly, each word has a value which carries some difference in the degree of approval or disapproval. On the side of isolation, the alternative labels could be *solitude, individuality,* and *independence*—which carry approval; or the label could be *withdrawal* or *alienation,* which carry disapproval. The idea of interaction can be rendered as *co-operation, interdependence, dependency,* and *inadequacy*—in a descending order on the scale of approval.

The framework of relationships is entered into when looking on families as having a unity which has its health and disorders. Here treatment is directed not to individual members, but to the family process. Group therapy of individuals who are deliberately brought together for the purpose of treatment also lies within this framework. The theory and practice of the treatment of families and of groups of strangers is dealt with in specialist literature. The references below are selected from a profuse literature on family and group therapy.[1] The field is growing rapidly and in such diverse ways that it would seem that all that many of them have in common is the label under which they operate. To some, family therapy means the rescue of an infant from

---

[1] DICKS, H. V., *Marital Tensions,* Tavistock, London, 1967.
FOULKES, S. H., *Therapeutic Group Analysis,* Allen & Unwin, 1964.
RICHTER, HORST E. (trans. by Denver and Helen Lindley), *The Family as Patient,* Souvenir Press, London, 1974.
SATIR, VIRGINIA, *Conjoint Family Therapy,* Science and Behaviour Books, Palo Alto, Calif., 1964.
SKYNNER, A.C.R. *One Flesh, Separate Persons; Principles of Family and Marital Psychotherapy,* Constable, London, 1975.
THOMPSON, SHEILA M. and KAHN, J. H., *The Group Process as a Helping Technique,* Pergamon Press, Oxford, 1970.
CROWE, MICHAEL, Conjoint marital therapy: Advice on interpretation, *J. psychosom. Res.* **17**, 309 (1973).

battering parents. Others seek the death of the family in order to prevent the persecution of a victim labelled as schizophrenic. Others again call themselves family therapists when they give separate treatment for individual psychiatric disorders of the family members. Finally, there is the psychodynamic view of a family as a unit which has its health and sickness and where the therapy is directed to the family process. Thus, at one extreme, the family is on the operating table; at the other, the family is on the couch! Theory has been borrowed directly from sociology, psychology, psychoanalysis, and from group psychotherapy. There is now an extensive literature which draws from systems theory and behaviour modification.

Group therapists have based their practice on individual psychotherapy, on sociometric techniques, on learning theory, and on existential philosphy, respectively. There are variations ranging from spontaneity in word and deed to carefully controlled and measured activities directed towards a predetermined aim. Group techniques are also applied in activity groups as a feature of structured tasks in craftwork or of leisure and artistic activities, such as sport and drama, and also of educational programmes.

The relationship framework also enters into some aspects of the treatment of individuals. Within psychotherapy, for example, account has to be taken of the individual's image of himself as a member of a larger group. Casework and counselling must be concerned with problems of personal relationships, and the needs of parents of handicapped children are a special case. A further example is the concept of transference and counter-transference. This is dealt with specifically in dynamic psychotherapy, but it is an aspect of every other professional encounter in any setting.

Beyond therapy, the relationship framework must be employed in the study of what occurs in conferences, consultations, and in the constructive and destructive features within small and large organizations.

Growth and Maturation

The use of the framework of growth is implied whenever the question of landmarks of development is raised. A mother asks, "Shouldn't he be walking now? ... talking?", "Should he be dry?", "Ought he to be able to read?" There is an expectation that certain functions should have been acquired by a certain age.

There is also the idea that certain stages of development are in themselves a vulnerable phase where instability is to be expected. People speak of adolescence and middle age as if these were the names of diseases.

It is thus necessary to be familiar with stages of development from a number of viewpoints:

(1) Norms of development have been derived from measurements of stages of growth and attainment of specific skills related to average ages. In this dimension one child is compared with a broad range of children of the same age.

(2) Notwithstanding the abstraction of norms of development referred to above, the different factors in the development of any one individual grow at different rates and, therefore, the progress in each of these factors may seem out of phase with that of the notional average.

(3) The average rate of growth in girls is different from that in boys.

(4) It is possible to study growth in terms of the sequence of the different stages in any one individual. In this case the enquiry is centred on that particular individual's history, and the stage which he has reached in his own personal development rather than on a comparison of his present characteristics.

(5) There is a widely held impression that growth ceases at the end of adolescence, when adult life is said to begin. This applies only to physical growth, which is limited by the completion of skeletal development (earlier in girls than in boys). However, intellectual and emotional development may continue in various ways throughout life.

(6) Biologically determined stages of development should be distinguished from the culturally or socially determined phases of life. For example, puberty is biological; adolescence is cultural. Middle age in men can be considered biological in so far as there is degeneration of physical capacity; in women there is also the recognizable end of the reproductive phase of life—the meno-

pause. In both men and women, however, some of the features attributed to middle age are cultural to the extent that they are mainly the fulfilment of popular expectations. Old age, too, has its mixture of biological inevitabilities and cultural variables. The adult life, between adolescence and middle age, is the least-studied period of life from a developmental point of view. In this respect it is almost the equivalent of the "latent period" of psycho-sexual development which, according to psycho-analytical theory, lies in between the complexities of the Oedipal stage and the storms of adolescence.

The comparison of adult life with the latency period is enhanced by the fact that the studies which have taken place in both areas have concentrated on performance—in one case at school, in the other at work.

It becomes evident that no diagnostic formulation within any dimension is complete without taking into account (a) developmental norms and (b) the stage an individual has reached in his own sequence of development.

Individuals vary in physique, height, weight, and body shape, and attempts have been made to base differences in personality features and temperament on the physical characteristics. There are extremes—dwarfs and giants, in which there are specific genetically based anomalies. Between the extremes there is a range of differences in the adult height of men and women, varying from tall to short. The pattern could be demonstrated by a normal distribution curve similar to that employed for the distribution of intelligence quotients. Thus, within the diagnostic framework, height, body shape, and other physical characteristics are sometimes factors in arriving at a specific diagnosis; in other cases it is part of a functional diagnosis; in others again, these characteristics are considered within the dimension of deviations.

What remains to be discussed is that there are occasions when growth provides a frame of reference of its own. Growth has its variations within the normal, comparing person with person and finding a place where one individual is measured against standards which apply to a population or a section of a population. This, however, is very different from taking stages of growth in the life history of a single individual and recognizing that these developmental stages are part of the changing image of that individual's own self and the image in other people's eyes. The quality of the image is a function of one's age and stage. Granted that there is an enduring quality of each personality, the value attached to the self varies according to the internal perceptions of the self and the worth given in the responses and communications of those whom the individual meets in daily encounters. Stages of growth are stages of development, and, at some particular point of disorder, the most important factor may be the perception of that individual's progress in terms of immaturity/maturity.

Within the frame of reference of growth there are interacting physical, intellectual, and emotional dimensions. The different tissues—skeletal, central nervous system, and reproductive organs—each have their separate rates of growth. Thus, (say) at the age of 14, boys and girls have reached differing proportions respectively of the final growth of the different tissues. It is impossible even to guess from the age of a person well within the range of normal how far that individual has progressed towards physical or biological maturity, or what that individual's place is in terms of sexual development.

There are expectations of behaviour which are entertained—amongst others, by parents and teachers—about the appropriate standards of behaviour for a child of a particular age or a particular height. If, for example, a child is taller than others of his age, he may be expected to behave in a manner appropriate to his apparent rather than his real age. There are other factors related to physical growth, but which are also associated with emotional development and interaction.

Within the maturational framework, it is also useful to recognize that the points of change from one biological stage, or from one cultural expectation, to another are as important as the stages themselves. Transitional stages have been envisaged as vulnerable points, or, conversely, as opportunities to transcend deficiences of the previous phase of development.

Crisis Theory

Crisis Theory[2] has been employed in order to bring professional help to individuals and families at these transitional stages which are related to personal development and to events within the family. Crisis

---

[2] See footnote on p. 71

intervention is a professional practice based on the idea that these are stages at which people can most effectively utilize help. A transitional stage in maturation, where the disturbances of adjustment have been successfully surmounted, provides an accumulation of strength for dealing with subsequent crises. In contrast, failure in one crisis is likely to increase the prospect of subsequent failure. Thus, the history of the maturational processes might give an indication of the kind and intensity of treatment required at some particular point of development.

Crisis theory has been put to good use in the normal transitional stages in order to help an individual pass securely from stage to stage. More specifically, it is invaluable in some of the hazards and emergencies which are unpredictable. Bereavement, the birth of a handicapped child, surgical operations, amputations, which occur in individuals, and natural disasters, which may affect a community, may call for, but not receive, appropriate help and support. It cannot be assumed that the usual professional routines cope with the disturbance of emotional balance on these occasions. The skill in intervention on these occasions needs its own theory to be added to what apparently is the main task.

We on our part stress that crisis intervention, which is described in its own literature as an independent process, should be looked upon as the utilization of one particular frame of reference, in addition to one's work in one or more other frames of reference, which have relevance to some circumstances in the life of an individual.

Psychosexual and Cognitive Development

Still within the frame of reference of growth, it is possible to select some aspect of an expanding theory of practice such as that of psychoanalysis. The historical model, which was one out of many created and utilized by Freud, takes the stages of psychosexual

---

[2] CAPLAN, G. *Prevention of Mental Disorders in Children*, Tavistock Publ., 1961.
CAPLAN, G., *The Theory and Practice of Mental Health Consultation*, Tavistock Publ., 1970.
MORRICE, J. K. W., *Crisis Intervention—Studies in Community Care*, Pergamon Press, 1976.

development as the channel through which we can trace backwards the sources of the normality and pathology of the adult. Psychopathological processes are identified with some particular stage of psychosexual maturation, in which difficulties occur and still continue to operate.

In Piaget's[3] cognitive theory, developmental changes in the organization of perception are related to each sequential stage from infancy to adult life. Gradually the child develops ideas about the nature of the outside world. New ideas are added to the existing framework or "schema".

A child passes from simple motor responses to stimuli, to intuitive and magical perceptions and interpretations. Next, he comes to have the ability to recognize categories of objects until, finally, the individual is capable of abstract thought. The importance of Piaget's work has been recognized in education. For our purpose, we have found it helpful to make comparisons of behaviour and performance, complained about in an older child, with that same behaviour and performance as a normal quality of a child at a younger age. Particularly with mental handicap, the measurement of performance against Piaget's developmental scale is more help than an IQ, and of more value than the diagnostic criteria of some category of mental deficiency. At the early stages of recognition of handicap, parents have a right to know what the handicap is, and this is where the diagnostic category comes in; at later stages they are concerned with what the child is doing and what capacity is yet in store.

We have passed rapidly through instances of theory and practice which utilize the framework of growth and development. Some of the schools we have mentioned (and there are many others) can occupy workers for their whole professional lifetime. We have attempted to put them into a general perspective with one another and with other frames of reference. Whichever approach we use, growth itself is assumed, but this cannot take place without the necessary supplies. This therefore is the next frame of reference for us to consider. The subject is so broad that even our brief account must be given a chapter of its own.

---

[3] PIAGET and INHELDER, *The Psychology of the Child*, Routledge & Kegan Paul, 1969.

8
The Primary Process of Provision

THERE is a vast literature dealing with the notion of deprivation, emotional and physical. One aspect of deprivation is separation from the mother, and nowhere in professional work with children has more emotion been aroused than on this topic. It is our contention that heated arguments take place when the subjects themselves contain elements in opposition to one another and when some components are hidden. Examination of the subject resembles psychotherapy in that one aims at revealing the hidden components.

Thus, deprivation and provision are two parts of one process of supplies that are considered to be essential; likewise, separation and union in family development are part of a dual process.[1] We believe that the most satisfactory way to examine and to discuss the theme of deprivation is to consider what processes are essential and, for that reason, this chapter is entitled "The Primary Process of Provision".

Deprivation and Provision

Provision is opposed to privation but not in the sense that normality is opposed to abnormality. Privation (lack) and deprivation (loss) are often used as if they were equivalent to some specific abnormality, so that one is asked for the "signs" of deprivation, its "causes" and "treatment"!

---

[1] KAHN, J. H. and WRIGHT, S. E., *Human Growth and the Development of Personality* (3rd edn.), Pergamon Press, 1980.

Many people lay the blame for all the troubles of the present generation on the fact that they have too much in comparison with the previous generation, who had a lower standard of provision. What is held to be lacking is the virtue that resulted from having to make do with less than one wished for. This is the reversal of the values that anything less than the optimum provision is considered to be abnormal. These two opposing views can be reconciled by the idea that growth takes place within an environment of provision, but that frustration can also stimulate growth. Privation and deprivation are relative terms, always used against a background of what is considered to be essential in a particular culture at a particular time.

There are three essential primary processes of provision—nurturing, teaching, and training—and, when these have been discussed, a fourth will be added.

Nurturing

The physical care which is given to the infant is usually provided in the first instance by the mother and is within the family. It consists of food, warmth, shelter, and protection from injury and disease; if these should occur, then the mother makes arrangements for treatment. These factors are concrete, but on their own are not sufficient for growth. They must be accompanied by love. To the infant, love means touching and being touched; it is the contact of skin against skin. It is by sounds, smells, and tastes that love is experienced. These early experiences lay down the pattern for future relationships. The infant grows to trust the mother, and later is able to maintain more abstract intimacies which can continue even at a distance.

The word "deprivation" is often used specifically in relation to maternal care. Rutter[2] has pointed out the difference between privation and deprivation, but absence or withdrawal of contact with the natural mother is described as "maternal deprivation".

Critics of the idea of the importance of continued contact of infant with the natural mother have argued the absence of a scientific basis for the views that separation from the mother is in any way harmful. If the

---

[2] RUTTER, MICHAEL, *Maternal Deprivation Reassessed*, Penguin, 1972.

term "maternal deprivation" is used to imply either a diagnosis in itself or a specific aetiological factor in a disorder in personality, there is a justification for some of the conflict that has been equated with "separation".

The conflict is resolved by borrowing the idea of simultaneous opposites which is expressed in the concept of the ambivalence of the individual.[3] In this situation the opposites are the different degrees of attachment, and the different degrees of individuality, that are appropriate at any one moment of life. At all stages there is some union or relationship with other individuals; at the same time, there has to be sufficient separation for the individual to have some experience of a personal self.

Bowlby[4] has drawn together the writings of various observers of infants brought up in institutions or with "mother substitutes" and related it to his own clinical experience. He emphasizes the ill effects in the long-term separation from the natural mother. Mary Ainsworth[5] went on to discuss the quality of mothering which is necessary in the child's original home or in any substitute placement. More recently Bowlby has concentrated on how attachments are made between infant and mother and subsequently other members of the family.

As with all scientific observations that go beyond simplistic equations, the observations require constant additions to match the increasing range of material which comes under scrutiny. Andry[6] brought in the dimension of relationships with fathers and showed that subsequent delinquency seemed to be connected with absent fathers rather than with "separated" mothers.

None of these findings should imply that family contacts should be uninterrupted over the 24 hours. In our present culture work is part of adult identity, and a mother of a young child who stays with her child may also suffer from separation from the varied rewards in her working life. Ever since the Industrial Revolution, a high proportion of mothers

[3] KAHN, J. H. and WRIGHT, S. E., *Human Growth and the Development of Personality* (3rd edn.), Pergamon Press, 1980.

[4] BOWLBY, T., *Child Care and the Growth of Love* (2nd edn.), Penguin, Harmondsworth, 1965.

[5] AINSWORTH, M.D., *The Effects of Maternal Deprivation*, Public Health, 1962.

[6] ANDRY, R. G., *Delinquency and Parental Pathology*, Methuen, London, 1960.

with dependent children have been compelled by economic necessity to take jobs outside their homes. Others went out to work by choice. There were few suitable occupations open to them and women teachers had to resign their posts on marriage! Richman[7] has shown that depression in young mothers is less frequent in those who return early to their working life. The issues are complex and there is no possible decision which does not have some disadvantages to some individual in the family network.

Yudkin and Holme[8] made detailed studies of child care in fatherless families and where the mother worked outside the home. They pointed out that the phenomenon of working mothers is not new, but once again is coming to the fore for three reasons: a greater equality in marriage, a longer working life for women after the reproductive period, and financial pressures with a desire for a higher standard of material provision for children. They spoke of the compromise mothers have to make between the choice of remaining in their own homes and that of following employment which has a satisfaction of its own. They highlight a neglected factor—the effect *on the mother* of *separation from the child*. Irrespective of the way in which the child thrives in someone else's care, it cannot be taken for granted that the mother can resume her contact at the level that the child has reached when restored to the mother's care. The mother has missed some stages of the child's growth.

Nurturing is given the first place amongst the primary processes of provision because without nurturing the infant cannot survive. Medical and social services can improve the level of health and the quality of life, but the first task of all is to ensure the physical survival. Within the present century infant mortality, which is the number of infants out of 1000 live births who fail to reach a first birthday, has fallen dramatically from near 200 to approximately 18—the actual figures varying in different localities in U.K.[9] There are African communities where the

[7] RICHMAN, NAOMI, Depression in mothers of pre-school children, *J. Child Psychol. Psychiat.* **17** (1) (1976).

[8] YUDKIN, S. and HOLME, A., *Working Mothers and Their Children*, Michael Joseph, London, 1963.

[9] KAHN, J. and WRIGHT, S. E., *Human Growth and the Development of Personality*, (3rd edn.), p. 84, Pergamon Press, Oxford, 1980.

nutritional shortages are such that one-third of all babies die before their first birthday. Thus nurturing is a family matter in the first instance and cannot be left to nature!

Teaching

Like nurturing, teaching begins in the family. It is the bringing of the perceptions of the outside world to the infant, familiarizing him with objects and people, and giving names to the objects and the people. The infant's world enlarges when he becomes acquainted with appearances and textures of the world around him; the sight, sound, touch, smell, and taste which provide a personal contact also build up a sensory world. The names are words which remain in the child's mind as symbols of the objects and people when these are no longer present. Object constancy depends upon verbalization. Some homes are poor in material necessities, others are poor in objects and names for them.[10]

Poverty in surrounding objects appears at its worst in the situation where an infant is lying flat in his cot with nothing to see but the ceiling. Unhappily this is still the fate of many infants in institutions and even in some homes. Schaffer[11] has noted that when a child is left outside in a pram the supply of stimulation is dependent on the adult, who must effect a change in the child's position in order to bring about a change in visual perspective. If the perspective includes a tree with leaves blowing in the wind the child's interest is captured. But an environment of profusion cannot be absorbed or recalled except through the medium of a name which allows the object to be separated out in the mind from the variegated background.

Teaching becomes professionalized within the educational system and, like nurturing, continues through every stage of life. This book is not the place in which to enlarge upon the theories of education, or upon the effects of compulsory school life on the child population as a whole.

---

[10] BERNSTEIN, B., Aspects of language and learning in the genesis of social process, *Child Psychol.* (1961).

[11] SCHAFFER, H. R. , Some issues for research in the study of attachment behaviour, in: B. M. FOSS (ed.), *Determinants of Infant Behaviour*, Methuen, 1963.

Training

The third of the primary processes of provision is the training by means of which the child receives the standards of the family and, indirectly, of society. Initially the infant cannot understand "do's" and "don'ts"; he knows only pleasure and unpleasure. However, the young child begins to adopt the family standards for fear of loss of parental love or for a wish to please the parent. Some actions are approved and others disapproved. Beyond this process of learning through reward and punishment (reinforcement and extinction) there is a constructive aspect in which the child spontaneously incorporates models of adult behaviour. These inner representations are the internal objects of the Kleinian school of psychoanalysis. Toilet training is one of the most important stages of a child's development and has to be left until an age when the child can understand what is demanded of him, and can have a wish to conform. As with perception, constraints are most effective when verbalized. By the time a child goes to school he has to some extent internalized the demands of his parents and these have become his own demands on himself. Freud has described this as super-ego development which has a verbal aspect. Confirmation of these ideas is unexpectedly provided by Luria[12] in a different theoretical framework. He studied intellectual development in children who were mentally handicapped, and he formulated ideas of the function of speech in regulating conduct. He uses ideas of "conditioning" in which, however, no account is taken of independent mental activity of the child.

We take the view that although restrictions appear to come from the outside world they are absorbed as experience of the child.

The idea of reward and punishment is part of the experience of life even to the extent that irrational conclusions are drawn about the workings of the universe. The scientific view of the physical world in its deterministic form is modelled on a particular version of man's perception of himself. The experience of reward and punishment for different kinds of behaviour has also led to ideas of moral determinism, which have been utilized in religious systems. There are, however, levels of modern scientific thinking which go beyond determinism and which recognize the element of chance. Similarly, in the moral and

---

[12] LURIA, R. A., *The Mentally Retarded Child*, Pergamon Press, 1963.

religious sphere it has been possible to abandon the ideas of a strict
balance sheet, and to recognize that there are experiences which do not
fit into the simple equation of a proportionate reward for good and bad
behaviour.[13]

Nurturing, teaching, and training have been dealt with as processes
essential for development. Their absence leads to ill effects and,
therefore, provision of any one of these elements is prescribed as if it
were a remedy for a disease, i.e. for something that has gone wrong. It
would be more appropriate to think of provision as being offered for
something that has not yet gone right. Not only are these things
prescribed as remedies, but any one of these three primary processes
may be chosen as the certain remedy for all the world's ills. Each person
has his favourite prescription, and this applies to professional workers
no less than to members of the popular world whose confidence is not
inhibited by scientific doubt. "I know what that child needs": one
person may say, "He needs love"; another may say, "He needs a better
school"; a third person may say, "What he needs is strict discipline",
or, putting it dramatically, "A kick in the pants". The love, the
teaching, and the training are indeed essential, but in conjunction with
one another. Love is not enough if given without opportunities for
intellectual development or without the restrictions necessary for
co-operative life. Teaching is ineffectual if given without love and
appropriate rules. Punishment in some form is inescapable, and may be
beneficial if given as an accompaniment to teaching and nurturing. It is
damaging if given without the assurance of love.

Essential though these three primary processes may be, there is still
something missing. Each of them is the gift of the present generation of
parents (and of society) to the younger generation. Each consists of
what has already come into existence. Nurturing offers the existing
resources; teaching, existing knowledge. Training offers the standards
in the possession of the present generation.

But change occurs—in resources, knowledge, and standards. Change
also occurs in the values which are attached to the different components
of these processes. Each new generation receives a share of existing
resources, knowledge, and standards, but also participates in and

---

[13] KAHN, J. H., *Job's Illness: Loss, Grief and Integration*, Pergamon Press, 1975.

contributes to the change. The new generation is, in part, the agent of change. There is, therefore, a fourth primary process, viz, experimenting.

Experimenting

The child is not a passive recipient of any of the primary processes of provision. At an early stage the infant learns how to hold milk in the mouth, to play with it, and either to swallow or spit it out—he has gained a choice. His experiments with the milk give him the capacity to refuse as well as to receive. The child begins to select perceptions to which he pays attention from others which do not seem to register. The movement of body parts can be enjoyed as a perception of the self. The first toy is some part of the infant's own body. Gradually, he learns how to play with toys which are external objects. The toy may have a shape which indicates a purpose in the mind of the adult who constructed it, but the child may use it for another purpose of his own contriving. Toy cars may be pushed along the floor upside-down without the use of the wheels, or piled on top of one another as if they were bricks. Building bricks can be used as cars, people, or blocks of flats.

A child may experiment also with words. Human speech is built up when the random sounds, which resemble adult words, are picked up and repeated by parents: the child reciprocates by imitating the sounds which the parents make as they teach the child the names of objects. The child, however, sometimes makes a mistake; mistakes are funny and people laugh, so the child makes the mistake again on purpose—he has learned to make a joke! Experiments with words lead to the discovery of unexpected connections between sounds and meanings. A pun is a discovery of resemblance between different words. Extempore play with toys can lead to the discovery of unexpected resemblances in the uses to which objects can be put.

A child also experiments with the standards given to him. He observes instructions at times, at other times ignores them, and, on occasion, invents rules of his own. By experimentation he explores the boundaries of what is permitted, and also becomes acquainted with what happens when he strays beyond the boundaries. He may discover that his experiments lead to an extension of the boundaries.

Experimenting with the primary process of nurturing, teaching, and training becomes an activity in its own right and is the fourth primary process of provision.

It has been stressed that the child is a participant in the receiving of nurturing, teaching and training. Conversely, parents are participants in the child's progress in experimentation.

A child will cease to experiment if every attempt is disapproved or feared. Permission to experiment is given only when the parent can tolerate something which was unanticipated. The parent's contribution is to be able to perceive something in the child's activity that is as fresh to them as it is to the child.

The adults' task is to validate the experiment and, on occasion, to add a little structure (but not too much) to what would otherwise be chaos. A child's first drawings are very much like scribbles, except that there seems to be some artistic composition in relation to the size of the paper. Gradually, the scribbles can contain some resemblances to familiar objects. If an adult shares in the drawings, the adult's efforts should not be too far ahead of those of the child. If a child is confronted with a perfect example to imitate, he gives up because the task is beyond him. When drawing jointly, the single dot or a line added to the child's product is better than a finished adult composition. Something can be adapted from Winnicott's[14] therapeutic technique of the use of "squiggles". It was his practice to use some scraps of paper, giving one to his young patient and keeping another for himself. Both would make a scribble and then exchange papers. The task was to add something to the other's effort, and it was a point of honour to find some meaning with the minimum of addition.

Many adults find difficulty in following the child's lead into unexpected directions. Parents and teachers alike may feel that they possess a quality of nurturing, teaching, and standards which is beyond dispute. The rightness is part of the quality. Some parents, for example, attempt to maintain consistency and uniformity with one another in the belief that this provides security. Complete uniformity, however, is never possible, if for no other reason than that one parent is a man and the other a woman. But it would be bad even if uniformity

---

[14] WINNICOTT, D. W. *Playing and Reality*, pp. 121–3, Tavistock Publ., London, 1971.

could be successfully achieved—in that case the child would be expected to be a miniature model of the parents in every particular, or be a rebel. If, however, the parents can allow themselves some variations from one another (within a broad framework of similarities) the child can develop his own individual qualities and still be acceptable.

Fear of External Influences

Many parents still attempt to control the sources of the child's nurturing, teaching, and training. They fear or resent other influences. In a one-parent family the fear of undesirable external influences may be greater than when two parents share the care of a child. But now it is no longer possible to exclude the intrusion of the outside world: a child no longer just has parents—he has a mother, a father, and a television set! From a very early age a child receives impressions and perceptions of life elsewhere.

One can only conjecture on the total effect of the amount and variety of stimuli which come to a child through television, but the profusion which exists adds emphasis to the fact that it is only possible to absorb a small proportion of the perceptions which impinge upon the senses.

The magical aspect of the sudden appearances and disappearances of people in familiar, and completely unfamiliar, activities on the T.V. screen is bound to make some contribution to ideas of human identity and capacities. The complexities of personal relationships may be presented faithfully or deliberately distorted. Information may be accurate or false. Events, whether disasters or momentous human achievements, are presented in rapid succession against a background of the daily routine of the home.

It is impossible to assess the way in which children (and adults for that matter) will utilize these perceptions and build them into value systems of their own.

Provision as Vehicle of Therapy

We have been at pains to distinguish the supply of primary processes of provision from treatment which is directed to a pathological state. In one case, what is being provided is the material out of which personality will be developed. In the other, treatment is directed to some part or process of the body after a diagnosis of disease has been made. The pathology is what has gone wrong and the effects of deprivation are seen in what has not gone right.

It has to be acknowledged, nevertheless, that each of these processes of provision can exist as an aspect of all kinds of treatment whether of diseases, dysfunctions, or deviations; and, when we pass from the diagnostic to other frames of reference, the continued optimum provision of the primary processes can become the main vehicle of the therapeutic process. There is a derivative of nurturing in the personal factor through which any form of treatment is conveyed. In psychotherapy and casework, the relationship of worker and patient is patterned on nurturing relationships even though the worker's professional skill adds a technical dimension.

Teaching plays a part in the therapeutic work in which attitudes are clarified and in which alternative ways of seeing and coping with problems are developed. Social work at ego levels deliberately accepts an approach through the intellect. In this sense the ego of the client is given the assistance of an alter-ego in the worker.

Training has its application in the forms of treatment which have a compulsory element exercised with legal powers. It also has a specialized aspect in "behaviour modification" based on Learning Theory. The name "behaviour shaping" acknowledges the way that this process differs from therapy which is directed to psychopathology.

Experimentation is a main feature of forms of treatment where there is no preconceived aim, and where the hoped-for result is the development of personality which goes beyond the patient's previously so-called "normal" state.

Psychodynamic psychotherapy, based as it is on the exploration of the balance between internal urges and external pressures, can have no predetermined final state. In this case the forces in the super-ego and id may receive precedence over ego factors.

We have discussed four primary processes of provision as being within a single frame of reference, and we have previously discussed three other frames of reference: diagnostic, relationship, and growth. It will be recalled that during the discussion of the diagnostic frame of reference, it was by adding the dimensions of dysfunctions and deviations to that of diseases that we were able to escape from the diagnostic framework and consider alternative frameworks.

Likewise, the expansion of the idea of deprivation into separate identifiable processes of provision can take us beyond the four frames of reference already outlined. Against the background of personal provision (in the absence of which the words "privation" and "deprivation" are used) there is the material and non-material environment. The word "environment" is used to include the natural resources which make life possible and provide some limits to human existence. The term is also used for the man-made modification of the natural habitat: water supplies, drainage, systems of agriculture, transport, and, in addition, the institutions and laws of organized society.

The whole purpose of elaborating the different frames of reference is to be able to find a theoretical justification for the different kinds of professional work which are undertaken for people and families. The aim is to help them with their *diseases*, *dysfunctions*, *deviations*, and *deficiencies* in essential needs. The general terms such as *problems*, *disorders*, and *difficulties* are used to avoid specifying the professional process which is employed in order to provide help. It will not be possible to be consistent, nor will it be possible to confine any profession within one frame of reference. Remedial work of various kinds can fit fairly readily into the frames of diagnosis, relationships (interaction), growth (maturation), or supplies (provision), but, in addition, some particular relevant aspect of the milieu is also selected for special attention. This external aspect becomes a framework of its own. Thus, the legal aspects of the care of children may be as important as, or more important than, the remedial work and, therefore, we speak of the statutory framework in contrast with the remedial one. The distinction is not always clear because on occasion a professional worker is himself the subject of statutory obligations to carry out particular functions on behalf of a child. A psychiatrist may himself be professionally obliged to use compulsion on patients under sections of the Mental Health Act, either for the protection of the patient or to protect others from the possible consequences of the patient's behaviour.

Within education it is the parents' obligation to ensure that the child attends school (or receives some approved form of education), but it is an obligation on the education authority to enforce the compulsion.

Professional workers are sometimes placed in the anomalous position of being uncertain whether they act on behalf of "society" or on behalf of the individuals to whom their work is directed. At the growing-point of the work of every profession an attempt has to be made to reveal the conflicts of interest in simultaneously existing opposing qualities—in the patients, in the professional worker, and in the organizations of society within which the professional work is carried out.

9
Occupational Hazards and the Double Bind

FREUD once referred to psychoanalysis as being one of the three impossible professions—the other two being teaching and government. The tasks are impossible, however, only insofar as the results achieved depend upon giving satisfaction to those for whom the tasks are undertaken! A good deal of work in the mental health services is in an even worse case—whenever anything is done, it is bound to be wrong! The reason for this is not merely lack of knowledge, lack of skill, or lack of technical resources—it is because, in addition to this lack, an expectation exists that the knowledge, skill, and resources actually are present. The failure lies in matching performance with expectation, and with the reciprocal phantasy of omnipotence and passivity.

The problem does not press hard on the one who provides the service if he himself has not accepted the expectation. In the first place, the problem is one of interpersonal relationships between those who provide and those who demand the service. In the last resort, the problem is one of inappropriate self-image of the worker.

In these situations, the mental health worker is doubly at a disadvantage. He is supposed to be an expert in problems of human relationships, and also he expects to be trained to understand his own inner mental life. Moreover, he is assumed to be able to identify, and cope with, any irrational aspects of his own responses.

There are a few familiar fragments of psychodynamic understanding which help the worker to deal with some of these issues. The patient or client may express the most bitter hostility, but none of this will touch the worker so long as he is able to believe that the hostility is the negative aspect of a two-sided transference relationship. The worker can explain to himself that these feelings are not directed at him personally; they are really attached to some other person in some previous situation. They are being transferred to the professional worker for the time being in a misguided way. Suitable interpretation will trace the feelings to the original source and the patient is freed from the tie to archaic situations. During this process, the worker on his part is relieved of the consequences of the immediate hate.

The concept of the negative transference has served the workers very well. On the patient's part, there have been many happy experiences which have helped the patient to cope with the realities of distressing current events. The results, however, are not always so happy. It is possible for the hostile patient to penetrate the professional armour, either by finding some entry into the worker's personal affairs or, alternatively, by fnding a way to diminish the worker's professional self-esteem. Michael Balint, in speaking of the analyst's difficulties with a group of patients which he identified under the label "The Basic Fault", described how the patient seems able to get under the analyst's skin. "He begins to know much too much about his analyst. This increase in knowledge does not originate from any outside source of information, but apparently from an uncanny talent that enables the patient to 'understand' the analyst's motives and to 'interpret' his behaviour. This uncanny talent may occasionally give the impression of or perhaps even amount to, telepathy or clairvoyance.[1] ...The analyst experiences this phenomenon as if the patient could see inside him, could find out things about him. The things thus found out are always highly personal, in some ways always concerned with the patient, and are in a way absolutely correct and true, and at the same time utterly out of proportion, and thus untrue—at least this is how the analyst feels them."

Ideally, even these personal attacks can be utilized as therapeutic material, so long as there is permission to discuss the possible meanings of the intercommunication, as there is within psychoanalysis. There

---

[1] See BALINT, M., *Notes on Parapsychology and Parapsychological Healing*, Int. J. Psycho-anal. Vol. 36, p. 18, 1955.

are, however, situations where such discussion is precluded and where pathology should not be imputed to the participants. These are situations in personal social life, in interprofessional communications, and in some of the interactions with colleagues.

Here are a few examples.

Request for Informal Advice

At a social gathering a fellow guest asks a question about a mental disorder from which a member of his family is suffering. Once the question has been asked, the worker is at a disadvantage from which he can never fully recover. The social role inhibits the pattern of professional response. The question may have been put in general terms, asking merely for knowledge which might seem churlish to deny. In a professional setting, however, the worker would be sensitive to the interaction of the family member with the person suffering from the disorder. If a few questions are asked which would help to concentrate the issue into manageable proportions, there is danger of usurping the professional responsibility which belongs to those in charge of the case. On the other hand, broad generalizations are either misleading or unsatisfying. Eventually, the questioner feels rebuffed.

The worker may also be left with the feeling that he has failed his profession by adding to the impression that it is impossible to get a straight answer from anyone connected with psychiatry.

Without making any assumptions about negative transference, there is plenty of hostility in everyday life which may originally centre on specific family relationships and which can very easily be redirected to members of professions who seem to come to the support of a troublesome relative. What seems to be demanded is either a simple answer which will find a cure or, failing that, an enthusiastic sharing in the condemnation of all those responsible for social and family problems.

A number of subtle assumptions underlie the communications on both sides and, amongst these is the belief that all mental health problems are easy, that mental illness is not like physical illness, that psychiatric treatment is a mystique, and that long interviews are unnecessary obstacles which could be avoided if one knew the right person or the right way round.

These conjectures are an indication that the psychiatric worker contributes to his own discomfiture by some degree of acceptance of the unsatisfactory nature of his professional work. He ought to be able to provide rational explanations of what he can and cannot do, but the explanations which come readily to mind are inclined to be platitudinous unless one is free to go beyond conventional boundaries of social conversation to construct an explanation which fits the particular case. Inevitably, once the question has been asked, the professional person is in the wrong. He may retaliate by putting the questioner in the wrong, but that would flout the courtesies of social relationships.

Personalizing the Question

A similar situation sometimes occurs during a professional interview with a parent whose child is mentally disturbed. "What would you do if it were your child?" Such a question would not be asked but for the assumption that there is an easier or better answer than the one which is being made available for that particular child. Perhaps there is also the thought that if the worker actually had such a problem in his own family he might be more sensitive to the distress in others. It may even be a wish to know that the worker really understands the nature of the problem. On similar lines is the question, "Have you ever had a case like this before?" Sometimes it is an effective reply to hazard guesses on these lines. But the answers never come easily, nor are they likely to be easily received. The questions are frequent ones. The answers vary according to circumstances. It could be said: "I hope I would do what you are doing now; that is, seek some professional help." On one occasion a parent took the point that, in that situation, the worker would be in the same position as he was. But such an answer should never be a routine. If it were, it would not have the advantage of being a spontaneous communication of immediate thoughts and feelings.

The Special Entitlement

In both instances quoted above, the discussion has referred to communication with relatives rather than to working directly with the patient. In both cases, too, there is an assumed equality between the enquirer and the professional worker. This situation also exists when there is a pre-existing relationship, such as with a colleague, a neighbour, a member of the worker's family, or with someone whose social standing is assumed to give special privileges. None of these situations would be a disadvantage if the person enquiring was completely uninvolved with the effects of the illness or, indeed, if he were not possibly some part of the interaction in which the disorder was expressed. The special position is not only held to be an entitlement to information and ready answers—in all sincerity, the special relationship is also thought to be usable in order to extract a better quality of treatment than does the standard product. The questioner does not conceal his position as an uninvited but equal partner with a professional worker, thereby separating himself from his original relationship with the identified patient.

The Special Patient

Main[2] has described in detail an extension of this problem when it is the patient who seems to have a special entitlement, either as a result of the pleas of the previous medical attendant or through some aspects of the patient's own personality and connections. Main was led to study the problem on account of the breakdown of a number of nurses in his hospital unit. It was the nurses themselves who were concerned about a number of their members who had been under obvious strain at their work. Dr. Main and a number of senior nurses met to discuss the matter, and gradually it became evident that the espisodes of severe individual strain, occurring over a period of 3 years, were connected with attempts to treat a few identifiable patients. Lack of success in treatment had been felt as failure as a person. "If only we had tried harder, or knew more, or been more sensitive, the failure would not have occurred." These patients, numbering a dozen in all, had features in common. There had been extreme pressure for the hospital to accept them. They were described as "worthwhile" and yet results of previous treatments elsewhere were all unsuccessful. They became known as "special patients", and amongst the nurses and doctors there was the

---

[2] MAIN, T. F., The ailment, *Br. J. med. Psychol.* **30** (3), 129–45.

feeling that these patients needed "better diagnosis, better interpretation ... more precise understanding". Some nurses and doctors selected themselves as having a special feel for the patients' difficulties, and a quality of goodness and sensitivity that was all important. The patients were protected from unwelcome hospital routine from which it was felt they should be exempt.

All these patients were given extra treatment sessions over and above the agreed programme of psychotherapy and, on the plea of the nurse, they were often given extra sedatives at night. The hospital staff separated itself into two groups—the "in" group who were sensitive to the needs of these patients and an "out" group who described them as "hysterically demanding". Eventually the patients' symptoms became so serious that they were too ill to be nursed in this open unit and were transferred to another unit in which physical treatments of increasing severity were applied. The final results were uniformly bad.

Main described the efforts to provide treatments so far above the ordinary that he eventually called it "super therapy". His paper, which should be read in its entirety by every worker in any mental health service, clearly shows that the short cut to better treatment leads to disaster. Good professionalism is a protection to both worker and patient. There is something fundamental in the urge to seek something better, and in the urge to provide it. There is also a narrow margin between the baby's cry which produces superabundant loving maternal care and the cry which evokes a battering.

The common factor in these situations is the attempt to bypass the professional procedure by appealing directly to the personal self of the worker. The stratagem is frequently successful because the professional worker is often prepared to concede a special position to those with family ties, friendship, and social links. There is, indeed, an etiquette by which members of kindred professions have a favoured status when in need of personal help and, therefore, there may be a willingness to save those in the special position from the frustration of preliminary enquiries, of waiting-lists, and the disadvantaged position of being subjected to questions without any corresponding right to question at the same level in return.

Many people in need justifiably resent the dependent position. It is true they have come for help, but they resent the price of placing themselves at a level of inferiority to the person providing the help. They find ways of

redressing the balance by gifts, favours, interesting pieces of general information, or even by solicitude for the worker's personal position. There are many ways, other than sexual, of seducing another person, and every one of them has at some time been employed. If the person seeking help succeeds in seducing the helper in any way, then all he is able to get in the way of help is something that he himself has envisaged. The helper, in gaining the satisfactions offered by the seducer, loses the capacity to stand apart from the situation. (Incidentally, one of the worst consequences of incest is that the parent becomes a supplicant to the child for the continuation of favours and can no longer offer the strength of parenthood.) Those considerations are extreme examples where, when getting something more than ordinary entitlements, the two parties become the exploiter and exploited in rapid rotation. What is being demanded, and being granted, appears to be something that is better than the service ordinarily available. But in the cases demonstrated by Main in the paper quoted above the patients eventually received something *worse* than the standard treatment. Professional rituals at least guarantee that the service never goes below the level of accepted practice.

Some conflict is present within the worker, and between the worker and the patient, in the attempts to provide a superior service. The conflict includes some additional participants, not physically present, but existing in the mind of worker and patient. The better service which is being offered represents a better doctor than the patient hitherto had, a better teacher, a better parent, or even a better husband or wife. The therapist places himself in open competition with one or more of these pre-existing claimants for the right to serve the patient. Sometimes the competition is with a figure from the past, and sometimes the patient remains the battleground in a contest in which he no longer needs to take an active part. One professional worker becomes embattled with another one over a patient whose own conflicts have quietly found a solution.

Even within the mental health professions there are many schools of psychiatry, psychology, and social work. Within the separate schools there are different versions of the original message. A mental health worker may find himself the victim, or the instigator, of intraprofessional conflict and battles of ideologies.

Family therapy, which is referred to elsewhere, reveals the conflict regarding the choice of professional procedures directed to personal factors in the family. The therapist redirects the emphasis from the patient to the family process. Some therapists enter the family situation in order to protect the identified patient from the harmful acts of the other members of the family who are credited with pathogenic influence. Conversely, some workers attempt to protect the remaining members of the family from the destructive activities of the identified patient. The worker, on his part, divides members of a family into those whose activities are hostile and destructive, and those who are victims or scapegoats; the family members, on their part, divide helpers into good or bad, i.e. sympathetic or callous.

The therapeutic process of family therapy depends upon the ability to explore family relationships, relating present events to previous experiences. Family therapy on these lines becomes impossible when the prospective patient has already had or gains access to the therapist's own personal and family life.

The Personal Level

The personal, social, relationship becomes a barrier to the intrusion of the therapist into hidden thoughts and feelings and to questions about details of family life. And yet, those who take advantage of these personal contacts feel that they ought to get all the benefits that a long-drawn-out, purely professional process might have yielded. The absence of a pre-existing social relationship makes it possible to use the interaction between patient and therapist as if it were a sample of relationships that exist elsewhere. The therapist who has a pre-existing *actual* relationship with a patient is denied the capacity to study the relationship at a transference level. How can we speak of transference in the presence of a relationship that is real?

Even when there is no pre-existing relationship, there are many potential patients who have social skills which provide a completely effective armour against entry into discussion of unwelcome themes. They make it their business to enquire into the background of the worker, to ask direct or indirect questions about his personal life and about members of his family, to find mutual acquaintance, and eventually to place themselves potentially in a social relationship with the worker.

This is fairly familiar ground to those working in services which are recognized as providing psychotherapy or casework on psychodynamic principles. If, at any point, the challenge shakes the confidence of the worker in the appropriateness of his techniques, he can examine his discomfort and share the knowledge of it with the patient as an additional dimension. This is the analysis of the counter-transference.

There are, however, many professional workers who have been trained in psychoanalytical principles and who subscribed to them, but whose work takes them into more open situations in community work where challenges cannot readily be sidetracked, nor can they be turned into grist in the therapeutic mill. A complex ambivalent relationship underlies many a brief encounter with acquaintances who have a similar social or educational background, or with people connected with professional or administrative colleagues. It is not permissible in these circumstances to refer to, or to discuss, the complexity of these feelings with those who do not come as patients. The mental health worker may well be put at a disadvantage when questioned or consulted outside the formal professional setting, but it is equally important to recognize that it is an imposition to use the assumptions of psychodynamic practice with colleagues who have not shared the pain through which these ideas were gained. It is worse still to open up the subject, and hint at the existence of solutions, in circumstances where time does not allow completion of the discussion, even if curiosity should be aroused.

Interaction with Colleagues

The next situation is that between colleagues, where one member of the staff of an organization feels that another member is behaving badly. It is tempting to speculate on the psychodynamics underlying the behaviour. There may be even good evidence of a recognizable syndrome of psychiatric disorder. In some cases it may be a good service to suggest that the staff member should seek psychiatric help, but equally it may be a dangerous suggestion to make. The behaviour complained of in one member might well be a justifiable response to the behaviour of the person who draws the psychiatric inference. There is clearly no authorization for psychiatric name-calling in quarrels of equals. But it would also be wrong to assume that all disputes are those of equals, or that members of a mental health organization do not have psychiatric disturbances. The counsel of perfection is always to treat the behaviour on its own merits without any interpretation and to leave suggestions of a psychiatric nature to come from outside the service. As in the situations previously discussed, all the parties concerned are the worse off for the attempt to use psychiatric themes without professional authorization.

Amongst colleagues, something is lost in personal professional esteem in these circumstances. Surely they of all people, whose work consists of dealing with conflicting relations, should be able to prevent conflict among themselves, or at least they should be able to deal satisfactorily with any disturbance that might arise!

The common factor in these situations is the mismatching of self-image and the performance which is expected. In conflicts between one individual and another, the framework is that of personal relationships. No one has authorization to step out of this framework into that of the encounter of therapist and patient. Conversely, within a therapeutic encounter there is no authorization to transfer to the framework of social life.

The difficulty is in the inappropriateness of demand and response. A question is asked within one framework and the answer is expected to be made within another framework, and there is no authorization to explore the motives which are presumed to lie behind the request and the response. It is the utilization in therapy of interpretation of behaviour, and the search for meanings and motives, that creates the difficulty in moving from one framework to another.

The problem does not exist if the worker can remain impervious to demands which appear irrelevant to the main purpose.

The problem does not exist in professions which deal with practical affairs, no matter how much they may be influenced by antecedent events. It is the practical consequence which is the objective.

The problem does not exist, even within psychiatry, social work, or education, if the communications are confined purely to so-called objective data.

The problems occur mainly in those who base their professional practice on theories about personality which apply as much to the worker as they do to those who are the subject of study and treatment.

It might well be thought that those who view psychiatric disorders as having a constitutional origin would be able to keep their own personalities detached from involvement with questions about their work. This is partly true, particularly for those who are able to limit their work to recognizable psychiatric syndromes where there is a clear division between psychosis and sanity, illness and health. Even those, however, who uphold the idea that all disorder must, in the last resort, have a physical basis, and who regard all psychiatric treatment as comparable with the treatment of physical illness, cannot exclude themselves from being consulted on problems of the upbringing of children, of education, of occupation, of the distress of marital disharmony, and of sexual anomalies. The solution may be to deal with complaints as if they were symptoms and the indication of some disorder. It then becomes possible to give *treatment* for the disorder. The disorder, when so diagnosed and treated, is something which stands apart from the personality of the patient and of the therapist and which may provide the token of authority for the therapist's work. There are parallels in social services where some material need, correctly "identified", gives the social worker the authorization to discuss problems of relationship, of aspirations, and of dissatisfactions and distress. Even without a theoretical basis for intervention into the emotional lives of individuals and families, many workers are able to give constructive help out of their experience of ordinary life. The doctor has this ability enhanced within the constant exchanges of views of his medical practice. The social worker, even when not embarking on social casework, makes comparison of patterns of living; the teacher has his experience of the differences between child and child, family and family. The response in these circumstances come from a purely personal accumulation of experiences, which, although derived in a professional setting, have no relationship to the original professional training. In that sense, responses come mainly from the untrained personal self and not from the trained professional part of the personality.

At some point in the treatment of emotional problems, even if they are given a label which is more appropriate to a physical illness or a material need, there are aspects which impinge on problems in the personal history of the professional worker. The worker may have arrived at some solution to these problems which is sufficient in his own life, but the existence of similar problems in patients constitutes an increasing challenge to the defences which protect the integrity of the worker's personality. It is never completely satisfactory to distort the nature of a problem in order to give acceptable shape to the professional response or to shelter the worker from the impact of the emotional factors.

Vulnerable Positions

There are numerous other examples where the professional worker finds himself at a disadvantage.

In general medicine, tradition has given patient and doctor some familiarity with what can be expected in the doctor/patient relationship. It is a popular notion that at one time there was general agreement as to the kind of complaint which justified the patient in calling for the doctor's help. There is also a familiar image of the kind of questioning and the kind of examination that the doctor made.

When social conditions alter, and when new knowledge puts the doctor in possession of new and unfamiliar techniques, there is scope for misunderstanding and mismatching of expectation. The conditions in the unspoken agreement can no longer be taken for granted; new negotiations have to be undertaken and explanations given (see page 10). The doctor may protest at having new duties imposed upon him, which may well have little relevance to his old training; the patient may feel deprived when old procedures are discarded before he himself has lost confidence in them.

A similar situation occurs with changes in educational practice and with changes in the way that material benefits are dispensed in the developing social services.

Workers in the vanguard of progress put themselves in a vulnerable position. If new ideas are introduced they are expected to be successful; and sometimes pioneers overstate the effectiveness of their work. Whereas traditional methods can have their failures, the critics of those traditional methods are not entitled to any. Thus progressive education (which by now has some traditional characteristics) is compared unfavourably with older methods if the behaviour or educational attainment of its pupils falls short of what is desired. Social work is now becoming the target of criticism of all those who are disturbed by problems of family life and social behaviour.

Dynamic understanding has been a growing-point in the professions working together simultaneously in mental health services and, therefore, it was part of the endowment which a number of social workers took with them into the newly created social service departments. The increasing levels of skill have been recognized by legislation which has entrusted the social service departments with responsibilities which were previously under the authority of the legal system. Social service departments, however, now find themselves in the position, through the Children and Young Persons Act 1969, of having to take a comprehensive responsibility for residential care and treatment of young offenders—even when without a full complement of skilled staff or sufficient residential places. The result is to receive blame for the failures and no credit for any successes.

In many of these cases criticism of the psychiatric and social work services is based on the belief that the problems on which they fail were previously dealt with satisfactorily by other methods.

The Double Bind

It is tempting to search for a developmental prototype of situations in which an individual is likely to find himself in a no-win position. The "double bind" as described by Bateson,[3] refers to the situation of a child with a parent, or of a subordinate with someone in authority. Questions are asked or some performance is demanded and *any* response is shown to be wrong. In its extreme form, as originally described, the double bind was believed to lead inexorably to schizophrenia. If *any* response is wrong, the best defence is to make *no response at all*. Gradually, the one in the inferior position withdraws into his own inner-mental life and finds satisfaction in a world of his own creation. This formulation has found its justification in the retrospective studies of some schizophrenic patients. The concept provides the basis for the use of the phrase "schizophrenogenic mother". Inciden-

---

[3] BATESON, G., *et al.*, Towards a theory of schizophrenia, *Behav. Sci.* (1956).

tally, it must be stressed that if this formulation is used about a schizophrenic member of a family where there is no justification for assuming that the aetiology lies in the family relationships, the result is to add further distress to parents who are already suffering the pain of having a sick child. The imputation that the illness is the result of the *hostility of a parent* can only be made in these terms in the presence of hostility on the part of the worker *towards* the parent.

The concept of the double bind has been amplified by Virginia Satir[4] and further elaborated by Kafka.[5] Satir describes how the effect of the double bind can be defeated. If an ambiguous request is made, it is not obligatory to search for the one correct meaning of the question before attempting to provide the right answer—it is sufficient to return to the questioner and ask for the meaning that was intended.

The double bind is a trap only when the one to whom it is applied believes that there is only one correct meaning and only one correct response.

Kafka makes the further point that the ambiguity can be an actual advantage once one relieves oneself of the burden of having to be right. The use of paradox can be an enrichment of meanings, and the ability to work with unanticipated responses can add to the number of new constructions of thought and behaviour.

A similar idea has been worked out by Hugh Kenner in a study of the literary work of James Joyce.[6] His thesis is that James Joyce became conscious of the utter failure of the so-called "objective" narrative style of the novel up to the beginning of this century. Clear logical narrative is unnatural, but it has been developed out of the idea that the "one word equals one thing". Joyce's writing recognized the existence of streams of consciousness which were free from the limits of strict time sequence and logical connections.

One can further add that fear of paradox, and refusal to perform anything which is not correct, will eventually stifle thought and inhibit originality. It is possible to be just correct enough, as is exemplified by the legal maxim, "De minimis non curat lex."

---

[4] SATIR, VIRGINIA, *Conjoint Family Therapy*, Science & Behav. Books Inc., 1967.
[5] KAFKA, J. S., Ambiguity for individuation: A critique and reformation of double bind theory, *Arch. Gen. Psychiat.* (1971).
[6] HUGH KENNER, *Joyce's Voices*, Faber, 1978.

It was implied earlier that the individual who allows the double bind to act adversely upon himself is escaping into an inner world of his own. At another level this may well apply to professions which are over-sensitive to criticism. Professions can have a private culture which is separate from the outer-world which does not understand them. When the profession is denigrated, a member gets support from the separateness and solidarity of the profession. But professions in their turn may also apply the double bind to consumers—there are those who find that the patient or the client is always in the wrong.

Sometimes humour is the means by which to bridge the gap between certainty and ambiguity. Jokes are tolerated ambiguity which permits new levels of communication. At its best level humour creates areas of agreement, and in any case humour can be a means of bringing hidden thoughts out into the open.

10
Psychotherapy and the Psychotherapist

THE name psychotherapy is given to a variety of methods of treatment which are mediated through the "psyche". The target of the treatment is the mind of the patient, and the instrument of the treatment is the mind of both therapist and patient.

Psychotherapy originated with the field of medicine, but nowadays it has many applications outside medical practice. Many of the practitioners have no formal qualifications and some appear to think that none are necessary. Medical training, in itself, is not sufficient, and it has been asserted that in the medically trained psychotherapists the original medical training has little relevance to the work; and yet where training for psychotherapy has been constructed for the purpose of the task, some of the ideas of healing derived from medicine have been introduced.

The different frames of reference which have already been referred to can carry ideas from psychotherapy into purposes that go beyond treatment, into the field of family interaction, and into ideas of maturation and the processes of development. Some of the ideas of psychotherapy have been added to activities which go by other names: "casework", "counselling", "remedial education", and more general terms such as "support".

Within psychotherapy there are procedures which owe their names to some special medium of communication which is used, and there are varieties of psychotherapy which are directed to families and to larger groups.

101

Psychodynamic Psychotherapy

The model on which the authors have been professionally nurtured is a psychodynamic brand of psychotherapy, originating with Freud, although some aspects predate him. The process is dynamic in referring to forces in the mind and using a variety of analogies which form models of the mind. The schools of dynamic psychology will be referred to later. There are also a variety of other systems each with its own theory.

Some of the theories which were worked out in the treatment of individuals have been adapted to the work with groups of individuals brought together for the purpose of treatment, and for the treatment of family groups who, in contrast with stranger groups, have a pre-existing and continuing relationship with one another. Group therapy and family therapy have, respectively, provided a crop of theories of their own. Therapy is also based on the theories of psychology of the individual or theory taken from other branches of knowledge and conjecture: from sociology, anthropology, economics, and even from the complex notions of higher mathematics. Cybernetics, for example, is a study of organization of human beings and machines.

Sources of Theory: Metaphors

We are taking the trouble to refer to a number of different sources from which theoretical models can be taken in order to demonstrate that every theory is in some sense a metaphor or figure of speech which is used to impose a pattern on nature where no satisfactory pattern had existed before. The pattern (and here we can borrow from classical Gestalt psychology) is a creation of the observer. Good patterns and good theories can be conveyed to others who are interested in the theme and who may add detail to the pattern or introduce more general changes into the design. There seems to be a general style of theories in each age with common features in the different sciences, just as in art. For example, Gothic style can apply to architecture, painting, and furniture design, with corresponding similarities in the Baroque, or Art Nouveau, or Art Deco styles. We are taking the general systems as an example of one which utilizes a current trend.

General Systems Theory

General systems theory, in particular, has been created and adapted to deal with the complex situation in which there are purposive individuals reacting to, and on, a living and non-living environment. It is an attempt to apply scientific principles, which were first created to deal with a simple mechanical setting, to living interactions. Within the framework of general systems theory, Hall and Fagen[1] have given a definition of a system as:

> a set of objects together with the relationships between the objects and between their attributes. The objects are the component parts of the systems, the attributes are the properties of the objects and the relationships tie the system together.

Yet general systems theory could be expanded and elaborated to embrace any of the theoretical and practical systems of psychotherapy to which we might refer. It has a special application to family therapy which was the first system of therapy to draw upon the vocabulary of the systems theory. This led Sue Waldrond-Skinner to various conclusions[2] in working with individuals and families: first, the individual's pain is reactive to a relationship; second, the relationship is current and ongoing and so, therefore, is the pain; third, the pain exists first in the relationship, then gets "located" in an individual who happens to form a component part of the relationship system, and finally, there is a circular movement, with a potentially infinite regress regarding the ultimate cause of the pain. Thus change, healing, and growth must take place within the system if the identified patient is to be rendered asymptomatic.

She goes on to outline some other premises of the theory. First the principle of non-summativity, i.e. the whole is greater than the sum of component parts. To treat the family system as "the patient" involves more than a diagnostic interest in the various members of the family. A second, important principle is that of homeostasis. Homeostasis[3] is

---

[1] HALL, A. and FAGEN, B., Definition of system, *General Systems Yearbook 1*, p. 18 (1956), quoted by HELEN E. DURKIN in *Progress in Group and Family Therapy* (eds. SAGER, C. J. and KAPLAN, H. S.), Brunner Mazel, 1972.

[2] WALDROND-SKINNER, SUE, Family therapy: the theoretical background, *APSA Proceedings of 10th Annual Conference*.

[3] Homeostasis is a term borrowed from physiology and refers to a tendency to restore any disturbance of the balance which is normally maintained in the chemical constituents of body fluids. There is constant change and sometimes the balance is seriously

maintenance within a system by the conversion of messages which come from the outside.

Positive feedback disrupts homeostasis. This is important if the family system is to be allowed to change and to grow. Negative feedback triggers the systems regulator, which by altering the system's internal condition maintains homeostasis.

Sue Waldrond-Skinner uses the term "homeostasis" as if it exists at different levels: at too high a level it produces rigidity and inflexibility and at too low a level chaos. Her third premise is that of circular causality. In the medical model causality is seen as a linear process. In general systems theory causality is seen as circular with no beginning and no end. Thus the current events of a family session are emphasized for both diagnosis and treatment rather than delving back into the past to link present to past retrologically (as in interpretative psychology). The whole circle of dysfunctional transactions between family members can be seen in operation. However, the family therapist does not as a rule emphasize the working-through process of dynamically orientated psychotherapy as a necessary perequisite for the maintenance of change. In other words, whereas dynamic psychotherapies originally were based on tracing present symptoms to their roots in the earlier history of the individual, family therapy is more likely to utilize interactions in the here and now.

Kleinian Concepts

In so doing, family therapists have to extend the application of some of the terms used in separate and precise ways in the different psychodynamic schools. The set of objects, for example, referred to in

---

disturbed, but it is *assumed* that a tendency exists for the balance spontaneously to be restored. The word "homeostasis" is applied to this tendency when it occurs. Thus it is a figure of speech or a convenient way of referring reassuringly to something which is assumed to be a property of the living organism. The word is similarly used to describe the balance between processes within the individual and the impact on these processes of forces in the outside physical world. When it is applied to family relationships, it is doubly an analogy, i.e. it is a term used as a figure of speech for the balance of interpersonal relationships taken from a figure of speech applied to changes in body chemistry. Having made this disclaimer, we are acknowledging the usefulness of the concept of homeostasis as used by Sue Waldrond-Skinner and we are including it in the outline which follows.

general systems theory could include the physical objects for which the theory was first applied, and also the internal representations of objects such as the internal objects of Kleinian theory: good and bad; part objects and whole objects; and also the structures of mind such as ego, super-ego, and id. In family therapy the *objects* comprise the total number of members of the family as defined for any particular purpose, plus the therapist(s). In individual psychotherapy, two objects, the therapist and patient, make up a system. The *relationships* are those of the current interactions of group members or family members with one another and with the therapist, as perceived in the reality of the here and now. The *attributes* are qualities which are applied to objects and persons according to each subject's previous experience. This would include the long-lasting stereotypes which family members apply in their perceptions and descriptions of one another, and it also includes the expectations and images of the therapist which pre-date the actual therapeutic encounter and which are carried into it. Thus the attributes can refer to some of the transference and counter-transference phenomena. Some psychoanalytical writings use the term "transference" to cover the actual relationship which develops between therapist and patients as well as the pre-existing images brought from previous experiences into the therapeutic sessions. This allows one to use each session as a sample of relationships present and past and other aspects of one's life. It applies to the individual patient, to the therapist, and it can be extended to the continuing relationships of family and of stranger groups.

The theme of general systems theory has been introduced as an example of a conceptual model which has facilitated the teaching of ideas about family therapy, and which can be applied also to individual psychotherapy.

The name "psychotherapy" was, at one time, applied to procedures used by non-Freudian therapists in order to avoid the specific label of psychoanalysis, which (when used strictly) applies only to Freudian theory and practice.

Psychoanalysis and Its Applications

The various forms of psychodynamic therapy (which include psychoanalysis) can be distinguished by the development of insight into the unconscious processes that accompany, or are responsible for, our illnesses. In order to achieve this it is usually necessary for the therapist to use the tool of interpretation. Insight, however, is not enough. The therapist aims at giving first understanding of, and then responsibility for, the symptoms to the patient. The patient's unconsciousness is enlarged and so is his responsibility and even, in some senses, his burden. In Freud's words, "Where Id was, Ego shall be."

The ego is enlarged, but we on our part also feel it is necessary to assert that the id is not diminished. The id, which is unconscious, consists of those mental activities formerly conscious and which become repressed. The id also includes creative forces which can give rise to ideas and activities which have yet to come into existence. This aspect of id is infinite, and no matter how much becomes conscious, it is not possible to comprehend that part which will forever remain unknown. When, in the beginning, Freud created the ego, the id, and the super-ego, he neglected to create the super-id!

For a description of psychoanalysis one must turn to Freud's own work and to contemporary presentations such as *The Technique and Practice of Psychoanalysis*.[4]

At first, psychoanalysis came to be applied, as a method of treatment, to particular disturbances. Hysteria, anxiety states, and obsessional and phobic states received the most attention. Psychoses were not exempt from study, and not only the depressive states, but also the delusions present in schizophrenia were shown to be comprehensible, even if the course could not, at that stage, be influenced.

Smail[5] has criticized the aspect of psychoanalysis which is reductive. He uses philosophical formulations, particularly of existential philosophy, to emphasize the living interaction. While acknowledging that the reductive process of tracing current events to past history has sometimes been applied mechanically, we on our part would stoutly maintain the importance of the past. In returning to systems theory, the idea of circular causality can serve us well at some points in treatment, but each person's history is also a linear process of development, with its sequential maturational changes and with the beneficial and

---

4 GREENSON, RALPH S., *The Technique and Practice of Psychoanalysis*, Vol. 1, Hogarth Press, 1967.

5 SMAIL, D. J., *Psychotherapy: A Personal Approach*, Dent, 1978.

damaging experiences which continue to exert their influence. The adult is not the same as the child, but there is a physical and an emotional continuity, and there are some enduring images of the past which remain and influence the present. The process of interpretative psychotherapy is more than a simple equation, such as Cause in the past = Effect in the present. It is the discovery of, and the expression of, the unexpressed part of a communication. In that sense it restores a balance and goes beyond the simple notion of homeostasis by creating a balance where none had existed before. Thus, when a patient continues to stress the horror of some present situation, one asks when something like this happened before. If the emphasis is on some past hurt, one asks what effect it is having on things happening now.[6]

Similarly, interpretation may explore and reveal the unconscious components of conscious behaviour, but there are times also when the therapist brings everyday reality, through a reverse interpretation, to those whose first communications are at psychotic levels. Thus critics of the historical aspect of psychotherapy have used too simple a model of what psychotherapy might entail.

At this point we wish to make clear that it is not our aim to condense the various treatises of the history, theory, and practice of psychoanalytical psychotherapy into a single comprehensive statement. The serious student practitioner of psychotherapy has to take the long haul of training and experience. But it is our purpose to show how the theories which are a constant preoccupation to psychotherapists affect every human encounter, whether professional, public, or private, and that there are occasions when the gleanings from psychotherapy are added to the general store of knowledge of human relationships. Transference and counter-transference are particularly relevant here. The term transference was invented by Freud. Following the experience of Breuer, who was the discoverer of the benefit that neurotic patients gained by an uninhibited recounting of past experiences, he actually became aware that some of the early sexual memories proved to be completely false. Moreover, Breuer's most notable patient brought her phantasies vividly into the consulting-room, and declared her belief

---

[6] KAHN, J. H., Do not interpretations belong to God?, *Br. J. Med. Psychol.* **48**, 227–36 (1975).

that he had made her pregnant. Breuer took fright and (significantly) went off on holiday with his wife, turning the patient over to Freud.

It was Freud's original contribution to be able to go beyond the content of the phantasy and to enquire why it was such phantasies arose. He was modest enough to exclude his own personal qualities as the originator of the phantasy and to search for some generalities of human thought and feeling. The word "transference" was first used for the carrying over or transferring to the therapist, or therapeutic situation, of memories and imaginings which had been experienced in the infantile encounters with the parents. Gradually the idea of transference became more comprehensively defined (and argued about) and the transference was no longer looked upon as an obstruction to the therapy, but rather as the main therapeutic tool. The patient not only brought memories of past events, but also brought a living re-enactment and elaboration of persisting methods of responding to complex relationships to which the patient seemed doomed. In this sense the use of the concept of transference bridges the historical and the existential models of therapy.

Transference and Counter-transference

The analysis of the transference becomes an essential part of, and some might say it is, the treatment. The counter-transference is a later discovery. The first notion was that the therapist, by reason of his own training analysis, was free of irrational thoughts. It gradually became apparent that no level of understanding and no amount of personal analysis can free an individual from linking current relationships with experiences in the past. Just as the patient, as one part, brings to the therapist his unconsummated experiences with parents and siblings, and with secondary transference figures (such as teachers, priests, and officers of the law, as well as various degrees of affectionate and hostile relationships in all the previous stages of development), the therapist, likewise, brings experiences of his own childhood, adolescence, and adulthood, and those of the uncompleted parts of his own analysis and of his encounters with previous patients. Patient and therapist bring their initial expectations to the first meeting and, going on from there, add fresh links between past and present. The therapist's expectations and distortions are referred to as counter-transference, and a large number of psychotherapists emphasize the necessity to analyse the counter-transference as an essential part of the treatment of the patient.[7] In order to facilitate the full flowering and ultimate resolution of the patient transference reactions, it is essential in all cases to recognize, acknowledge, clarify, differentiate, and even nurture the non-transference (or relatively transference-free) reactions between patient and analyst.

Self-disclosure

Weiner[8] describes the range of self-disclosure as ranging from neutrality to nudity. At one end would be the psychoanalysts who remain a blank screen onto which the patient can project his phantasies and, at the other, would be the exponents of the newer therapies, some of which encourage complete openness on the part of the therapist. There is a place in psychotherapy or casework for the therapist to be genuine and not to hide all aspects of himself. The patient will anyway have made some deductions from the way in which the therapist is dressed, or what car he drives, or in what accent he speaks. Thus no therapist can be completely anonymous. Nor would he want to be, because to show concern and be genuine with a patient is an important aspect of the work. This does not, however, mean one must reveal private thoughts.

---

[7] We have emphasized the initial expectations and distortions in transference and counter-transference which go to form the irrational part of the therapist/patient relationship. Some writers use the terms "transference" and "counter-transference" for the whole of the relationship, which includes both positive and negative elements of the actual relationships which develop between individuals who have prolonged contact with an agreed aim. Some writers distinguish the realistic aspect of growing complex relationships with other terms, such as "working alliance" (GREENSON, RALPH R., *The Technique and Practice of Psychoanalysis*, Vol. 1, Hogarth Press, 1967) or "libidinal transference" (SLAVSON, S. R., *Analytic Group Psychotherapy with Children, Adolescents, and Adults*, Columbia University Press, New York, 1956). The analysis of the counter-transference requires frankness on the part of the therapist and imposes a duty on him to respond interpretatively to a communication which he might have made a few minutes, or a few sessions, previously. A therapist's disclosure is a complex and contentious theme.

[8] WEINER, MEYRON F., *Therapist Disclosure—The Use of Self in Psychotherapy*, Butterworth, 1978.

Privacy and Secrecy

There is a move afoot, especially amongst certain family therapists, to expose the secrets of a family to all the members of the family. In our opinion, this does not mean that private matters of any members of the family should become public property of the other members. We should distinguish between privacy and secrecy. Secrecy implies guilt attached to the thought and event and, as such, may interfere with the individual's capacity to relate to members of his family, or to friends outside the family. Privacy is necessary for everyone. However close a relationship might be, there will be areas of both psychic and physical life which are not shared and remain the private concern of the individual. Just as this is true between adults, it is true in a family where both parents and children have areas of life which remain unshared. Moreover, we would give support to each individual's claim to some areas of privacy. This is also true for the therapist in relationship to his patient.

But who decides what is secrecy and what is privacy? At some point every therapist will be accused of tantalizing the patient by not giving a straight answer to a simple question about his personal life. We have already referred to the degrees of self-disclosure, but it more difficult to find the theoretical grounds on which distinctions are made between secrecy and privacy. We should also record the firmly held view of some therapists that every question should be answered with the question, "Why do you ask?" There are, in contrast, many therapists who give a simple factual answer to a question on a matter of fact, such as, "Where do you live?", "Are you married?", "How many children do you have?" A simple answer may be left at that, leaving the patient to make interpretations as to how welcome the question was.

The question and answer may reappear in further communications. If the question refers to the therapist's own personal sexual relations, the answer is not the property of the therapist alone. An answer includes something of the privacy of others involved in the therapist's relationships. It goes beyond the theory of transference and counter-transference relationships, and we hold the view that privacy is also an obligation to preserve his own and other people's secrets. If any guilt attaches to these secrets, the guilt is not a relevant theme in the communications with a third party.

Physical Contact and Surrogate Roles

The question of physical contact with a patient is an area of even greater controversy. The touch of the hand often conveys a genuine warmth of feeling and understanding. Shaking hands with a patient on meeting and parting may be a conventional courtesy and be accepted as such. There are also physical contacts which are meant to be the communication of affections as well as concern, and there are contacts where the erotic content is plainly to be seen.

Some therapists openly utilize physical contact for its erotic component, and there are many cases where the simple touch or handshake is given the erotic content by the patient, even when this was not consciously intended on the part of the therapist. Every contact is open to a variety of interpretations, and in some cases these interpretations are made. We do not propose to discuss, at this point, encounter therapy, where the contact is the medium of treatment. We would merely ask the intending therapist his image of himself which he has transferred from other situations. At all times, therapy is in the image of some previous relationship. The therapist perceives some of the patient's needs and tries to supply them. Patients have had parents, teachers, doctors, priests, lovers, spouses, children, and some of these (or all of them) have failed the patient. The therapist may, in recompense, try to be a better parent, a better teacher, a better doctor, a better priest, a better lover, a better spouse, a better child than any that the patient had previously. We might add that he sometimes tries to be a better policeman. When usurping these roles (and thereby giving expression to the counter-transference) he is likely to do something which is counter-productive, or even damaging.

All these surrogate roles have their dangers, and the warning against the utilizing of the need for physical, erotic activity should be taken seriously. Love does not cure in the unequal circumstances of therapist and patient. If equality is to be attained, the therapist must forgo his therapeutic role. This applies both ways: the patient who wishes to actualize his love for the therapist must forgo the role of patient. It only remains to add that every one of the surrogate roles will exist at some time in the mind of each, and the analysis of the transference and counter-transference is to interpret them. The interpretation does not destroy the growing, affectionate, and sometimes hostile relationship which forms the bond during therapy, and which is likely to survive as good feeling when the treatment is concluded.

Jenny M. Lewis[9] lays down guidelines for students of psychotherapy and casework on the decision to disclose personal material. We have selected the following statements from her work:

(1) The therapist can be genuine and be himself or herself in the course of psychotherapy without disclosing material of a highly personal nature.

(2) The more urgently a therapist feels the need to disclose, the greater the need to consider carefully the reasons for the proposed disclosure.

(3) When the therapist experiences intense feelings in the psychotherapy sessions that cannot be hidden, and the patient notes them, they should not be denied.

(4) Errors on the part of the therapist should not be denied.

(5) No disclosure should be made without giving consideration to the most probable impact on the patient.

We would infer from Lewis's formulation that the disclosures are often made by therapists for the therapist's own personal reasons and may be more of a burden than a help for the patient. To this proviso we should add that, when the therapist can share his accompanying thoughts with the patient and his own communications, he is often reaching the highest levels of therapeutic potential.

In actual clinical practice of conjoint therapy, where two or more therapists are conducting the treatment, we have noted an unexpected therapeutic bonus when we have contributed to the session a remark that hitherto we would have exchanged amongst ourselves after the session. Perhaps this is what family therapists are getting at when they refer to themselves as being caught up in the family system.

---

9 LEWIS, JENNY M., in WEINER, MEYRON F., *Therapist Disclosure—The Use of Self in Psychotherapy*, Butterworth, 1978.

11

Care and Support: For Whom?

Categories of Care

Care is one of the catchwords of the medical and social services. One speaks of child care, residential care, community care, and, in medicine, care and treatment. It is also part of the aim of the education services to offer care as well as teaching.

Caring is a part of every kind of treatment and, although caring is highly valued, no one ever teaches a worker how to care. When professional skills are directed to some precisely defined objective the caring is an accompaniment. When the skills fail or are inappropriate, the caring is all that is left. But it is too much to ask that this non-specific caring can be offered to everyone whom the worker encounters.

Paradoxically, the cases which are most difficult to treat are the ones likely to be allocated for "care" to workers with the least training and experience. When the diagnosis is clear, and where the treatment follows logically from the diagnosis, the cases fall naturally to the professional service in which skills have been developed—presumably skilled workers do not "have to" care.

It is for that reason that cases which elude precise diagnosis, and for which there is no agreed treatment (even though the seriousness of the case is not in dispute), are inclined to fall to generic services and to be allocated to the most recent recruits.

A clinician feels secure when the diagnostic label which he uses makes a difference to the treatment which he gives. In many of the conditions for which people seek help, treatment may be encumbered by the activities of a number of other professional services. There are many who are already involved with the child at school and with the adult within a network of social and environmental services. Ideally, if there are several services involved with the same individual (or family), and possibly with the same problem, the justification is that each has a special way of looking at the problem, and this insight leads to a special way of helping with the problem. It is the particular—even exclusive—contribution which allows a professional service to develop an area of accepted responsibility. The individual comes with problems, but the workers within the professional service have problems if what they have to offer does not seem to fit what seems to be required.

Support

One way of dealing with this problem is to reject those who do not fit in with the available skills. Some psychotherapeutic services are able to define those cases which are suitable for treatment and to turn away those cases which are not suitable for treatment. Another solution to the workers' problems was to offer something *apparently* non-specific and, for want of any other label, the process which was offered was called "support". In fact, at any point where it seemed difficult to say what should be given a ready answer could be found in the term "give them support". When the word "support" is used, it is implied that no further definition is necessary. It is not psychotherapy; it is not the giving of material help; it is not the teaching of some skill. Support, however, when eventually defined, could be seen to be an accompaniment of any of these activities.

Let us take an actual incident where, at the end of a case conference, the final agreed decision was that the patient should be given support. Out of pure awkwardness one participant of the conference asked, "What will we be doing when we give support?" No one could answer and the question was then considered to be destructive. After all, the workers were all experienced and there was no reason to doubt the value of what they did. But the unanswered question left some turmoil in the minds of the participants.

Finally an answer emerged:

> Support is doing *nothing* when it is not necessary to do anything, so long as the person giving the support has the resources and the skill to do *something* when it is necessary to do something.

Support, therefore, is a constructive way of standing by, with the skill and preparedness to do whatever might become appropriate. This might be the application of some skill, or the provision of some resource which is in one's own possession. Alternatively, it could be the knowledge of how to gain access to skills and resources that are in the possession of some other services.

Support is also the refusing to do anything which might be without benefit or even harmful. Thus, support is the constructive withholding of activity, together with the holding of one's self in readiness for any activity which might be required.

A simple example will illustrate a number of points. A colleague once described the experience of tripping over the edge of the pavement in a busy town thoroughfare. He fell flat on the pavement, winded, and momentarily immobile. A woman who was passing by stopped close to him and asked, "Are you all right?" He replied, "I think so." She continued, "I will stand here until you are ready to get up." After several seconds (which seemed a long time) the colleague drew himself to his feet and dusted himself down. The woman again asked, "Are you all right?", and this time he replied with a simple "Yes". She said, "Good morning", and he said, "Good morning", and they walked off in different directions.

While he was on the ground she did not hold out her hand to him, nor did she encourage him to get up. Rather did she imply that she would stand between him and the busy throng, so that he could take as long as he wished in order to recover himself. It was also implied that if he had been hurt, and had needed any kind of help, she would have been able to organize it. The exchanges were completely adequate to the circumstances, and neither of them seemed to wish (or to need) to use the opportunity of this chance encounter for any other purpose. Neither of them said, "Let's go and have coffee" (and after that, who knows what else?). The encounter was not used to satisfy a feeling of loneliness in either party. There was no need to turn the occasion into an opening for the satisfaction of any previously felt need; neither needed to exploit the other. No attempt was made to deal with any additional factors which, in other circumstances, might have been considered relevant. There was no need to ask why he had fallen, nor to enter into any of the personal and interpersonal issues which might have made him vulnerable at that particular moment. It was taken for granted that the accident was recoverable without any further enquiries or treatment. But if that assumption should prove to be unfounded, another line of action could be taken as and when it should be required.

Holding and Withholding

This was support which had the two opposing qualities of holding and withholding. The holding was at a physical distance, but the potentiality of actual contact was there. Even at that level it resembled the physical contact which the mother is able to give a child who is hurt. The holding in this case gave potential physical support in the temporary distress. The withholding was demonstrated by what was *not* done. No unnecessary treatment was carried out, nor was there any gratuitous offer of external resources. It was implied that there was confidence that the internal resources would be sufficient, if given time. The gift was the gift of time when time has value, and when the time can be used for a practical purpose if it should be necessary.

Those whose job is to offer help also have occasions when they themselves need help. The staff of professional organizations need someone to turn to—someone who has the time to respond. The support which professional staff should receive from their superiors, supervisors, and colleagues will also depend upon the ready availability of additional skills as well as time. In this situation support is not just encouragement and reassurance, nor is it a collusive approval of whatever might happen to have been done. Support requires some discrimination as to the value of any possible alternative decisions and, therefore, it requires the ability to make a professional appraisal of the activities which are being undertaken. Support also includes the caring for the worker as an individual and as a member of a service, and as someone with whom it is worth while spending time.

Another aspect of support (whether for patients and clients or for staff members) is the process of listening—not just listening and saying nothing, but listening with the capacity to discriminate when it is necessary to say something and then to say it. Thus listening is saying nothing that arises out of one's own needs, but it requires a sensitivity to detect the exact moment when a response becomes necessary in the interests of other parties. This also is the gift and the use of time.

The holding or the withholding is an experience for both parties. There are many occasions in which the perception of either component by the recipient is of anything but support. Holding may seem to be an intrusion into one's autonomy; withholding may seem to be a denial of some service which is a clear entitlement. The giver of the support is expected to have the capacity to discriminate regarding the expected benefits from each of the two components and to have confidence that withholding is appropriate and tolerable or that holding is not an intrusion into the personality of another individual.

The processes of support, like the communications in psychotherapy, have to be newly created at each encounter. The one offering support has to be able to tolerate a response which is unanticipated and possibly better than any response that he himself might have had in mind. The giver of support has to take risks—he is using communications which are full of ambiguity, and the choice either of holding or withholding is an alternative to the bringing in of specific technical skills.

The switch from a therapeutic role to that of giving non-specific support may be disturbing. All credit is due to those who enter the "caring" professions in the hope of finding ways of relieving suffering. People who face threats from within their own personalities or from the outside world need the comfort of the belief that help will be forthcoming. The therapist needs the support of a belief that help is his to give. If the therapist has nothing to give but his skill, and if his effectiveness should then fail, he may, for a time, find consolation in the thought that his actions were technically accurate; but eventually he begins to question the theoretical formulations which gave him his professional identity.

Professional Despair

There is a climacteric in the life of many professional workers when helpful illusions no longer operate. Some workers are able to maintain their youthful optimism throughout their careers and, indeed, their entire lives. In other cases, the impression of fading capacities takes the shape of professional despair, but even this can lead to new insights.

Professional development follows a similar course. New entrants to a profession make a contribution through their interaction with those who brought the professional family into existence. The main theories employed by the professional come into being, develop, change, and eventually cease to exercise their original power. Psychodynamic procedures lose their potency unless they are renewed by the thinking of successive generations.

The dissatisfaction with the original formulations comes best from those who are its pioneers. When Freud[1] wrote *Analysis—Terminable and Interminable* he was able to express some of the pessimism of one whose success had given every justification for the belief that human beings can bring some understanding and relief to one another's distress. He had reached the position where he was able to recognize the powerful resistance to change—even to changes which are intended to be for the better. He had also learnt to recognize that analysts in their own personalities did not invariably come up to the standards of psychological normality to which they wished to "educate" their patients. He had begun to recognize the superstitious beliefs of mankind which remained as residues in all strata of society. Only a portion of the mental activities could be touched by the therapeutic efforts.

The Basic Fault

We have already referred to a theme in *The Basic Fault* by Michael Balint.[2] He attempted to identify the characteristics of those patients who pursued their analysis with a display of eager co-operation, but who remained blithely untouched by any interpretation. There had

---

1 FREUD, S., 1937 Standard Edition, Volume 23, pp. 216–53, Hogarth Press, 1964.
2 BALINT, M., *The Basic Fault*, Tavistock Publ. 1968.

always been patients whose treatment proved to be difficult or unsatisfactory, but it had been hoped that improvements in techniques would eventually bring them within the range of the psychoanalytic effectiveness. Gradually Balint found it necessary to abandon the hope of the ultimate perfectability of therapy and, instead, to study the nature of the difficulty.

Every therapist had his residue of patients described as "deeply disturbed", "profoundly split", "severely schizoid", "weak ego", "highly narcissistic". The therapist sometimes attempted to find reassurance for himself by explaining failure in terms of strengths of resistance.

Balint took his study into the infantile developmental levels which seemed to be operating. Interpretations were ineffective because of the inadequacy of adult language for communication. The disturbances had taken place at a more primitive level than that of the oedipal situation, and he called it the level of the basic fault. At this level, which corresponds to the primary object relationship (described by him elsewhere[3]), there is only room for two persons, in contrast to the oedipal level in which there is interaction between three individuals. In the primary two-person relationship, which is represented by the first contact of mother and child, satisfaction comes from the "fitting in" of the external object with the needs of the subject. Frustration is the result of the slightest failure to fit in with the subject's self-perception.

When the level of the basic fault is engaged, the atmosphere changes. The interaction does not reach the level of a transference phenomenon in which parallels can be drawn from previous situations—it is only the present that counts. The analyst's interpretations are interpreted by the patient as an attack, a demand, a base insinuation, uncalled-for rudeness, unfair treatment, injustice, or lack of consideration, affection, and love. Ordinary words which previously had had an agreed conventional adult meaning become important and powerful in either a good or a bad sense.

In other cases, the analyst's failure to make an appropriate response does not produce a reaction of anger, but rather a feeling of emptiness, being lost, deadness, futility, and a lifeless acceptance of everything that

---

[3] BALINT, M., *Primary Love and Psycho-analytic Technique*, 2nd edn., Tavistock Publ., 1952.

is offered. The desperation and hopelessness lead to inordinate demands which Balint called oral grief.

On occasion, an even deeper level seems to operate, described as narcissism, which, paradoxically, is an area of potential creativity. It is at this level that some highly talented individuals can pursue their objective regardless of the needs and suffering of any other individual. Beneath the two-person relationship is the one that can include none other than the self.

None of these phenomena are restricted to the interaction between analyst and patient. They are a not uncommon feature of family life, or interactions of colleagues and of occupational groups, and they may be a feature of the relationship between any professional worker and his client.

The term "basic fault" has a double meaning. The "fault" is a split which penetrates the deepest geological strata, and, by analogy, the term is applied to the human personality. It also refers to the way in which the patient convincingly puts the blame or fault on the therapist.

Therapeutic Impasse

The same theme was taken up by Giovacchini,[4] clinical professor in the Department of Psychiatry at the University of Illinois. He discussed patients who were difficult to treat, not because of difficulties which could be remedied by better interpretative and therapeutic techniques, but because of the fact that they passed beyond therapeutic tolerances. The therapist arrived at an impasse.

Giovacchini began to identify specific types of "characterological pathology". These patients appeared to provoke the therapist to become critical and irritable, even though they themselves were helpless and vulnerable. Tape recordings of interviews were examined and they showed that these patients constantly blamed outside forces for their problems. Something traumatic had occurred to them, and everything had to be understood in these terms. When the therapist attempted to explain that the patient was now creating his own

[4] GIOVACCHINI, P. L., Technical difficulties in treating some characterological disorders: Counter-transference problems, *Int. Psychoanal. Psychother.* 1 (1), 112–28 (1972).

difficulties by provocative behaviour, the idea was strongly resisted. The therapist now became the representative of this traumatic external world.

The therapist began to feel that his professional integrity and value systems were being undermined. The process took place insidiously. If there had been delusions or craziness, the therapist could have felt comfortable. The apparent rationality of the patient was the discomforting factor. Eventually the therapist realized that the patient treated him as if he did not exist.

The patient's thinking was described as being mainly concrete and non-psychological, i.e. "devoid of feeling, imagination, and ability to scrutinize emotional nuances". The therapist was denied the kind of satisfaction which can be present when working with a negative transference so long as one is confident that it *is* a transference.

Giovacchini concluded that "those potentially disruptive reactions can lead to valuable insight" in that they are replicas of early developmental phases and infant/parent constellations. One can only add that at times this valuable insight is bought at a very heavy price!

The same phenomena have been given a more general discussion within a sociological and social work dimension by Norman A. Polansky, who was professor in the School of Social Work at the University of Georgia, U.S.A. In a paper, "Beyond Despair", delivered to the National Institute of Social Work Training, London, in May 1973,[5] he described his concept of alienation. The "feelings of powerlessness, meaninglessness, normlessness and vagueness are antagonistic to the expectability which forms part of the measure of sanity". Depression still retains some logic, but the schizoid state is beyond logic and beyond determinancy. In the schizoid state the therapist feels gradually to become destroyed because he is irrelevant.

Polansky described the futility and detachment which had become a characteristic of contemporary culture. The schizoid person withdraws into the emotional void inside himself. It is worse than depression not to feel anything at all. The condition is beyond the reach of psychoanalysis which assumes that behaviour can become understandable

---

[5] POLANSKY, N. A., Beyond despair, in *Shaping the New Social Work*, (ed. ALFRED Kahn), Columbia Univ. Press, 1973.

and therefore acceptable. The treatment problem is that the therapist begins to experience a feeling of futility, detachment, and alienation. The description recalls Giovacchini's experience that the patient made the therapist feel to be a "non-person".

This condition, whether it be represented in the community at large or by a therapist in a consulting-room, can only be achieved after some success has been obtained. The therapist, becoming accustomed to the benefits of his increasing skill, is surprised to find areas which he cannot penetrate.

Loss of Illusion

There is a parallel in the condition of some successful professional and business men, and some politicians, who seemingly achieve their ambitions only to find that satisfaction still eludes them. Why should an experienced professional worker, with the reality of a past of successes to his credit, ever fail? The failure is an injury to the growing belief in his own omnipotence. The situation is a product of the lengthening of the span of life, with survival past the time when the peak of capacity has arrived. When death occurs while a person is still advancing there is no problem.

At a national level an industrial society gives a proportion of the population a prosperity which offers only a limited satisfaction. Wealth does not necessarily give security. When any setback occurs after the enjoyment of prosperity, the quality of the reaction varies with the level of infantile experience which is reactivated. If the depressive position is revived, there is a loss of the illusion of future fulfilment; the more primitive paranoid position is likely to be revived in those persons where fulfilment has never been enjoyed in the past.

Many people look back to the time when reassurance was gained from the tie to the family. There was confirmation of the worth of one's own self from the goodness that was perceived in the surrounding family. If, however, the concept of family no longer carries the idea of goodness, then no cure is to be obtained by therapy which is directed towards the family processes. There seem to be two opposing views about family therapy. The first is that the family is the source of disturbance and must be destroyed. The second is that the individual can draw upon the family processes and, therefore, the family breakdowns can and should be repaired.

Similarly, there are two ideas of sociopathology. The first is that individual disorder is the result of pressures from a society which should be destroyed. The second is that the disorder represents an alienation from beneficial contact with other individuals and, therefore, treatment should take place in a group which is a miniature representative of a larger society.

In the various frames of reference that have been previously outlined there is always a tendency to use false analogies from the medical model: pathology and cure. Cure is not always obtainable despite all the advances in knowledge. Each frame of reference can be utilized in order to deal with the processes and activities which are within its scope. When cure is not obtainable, treatment can be offered in response to a perceived need, and not for any pathology which may seem to be there and yet inaccessible.

Targets of Treatment

The treatment should be a provision which is offered for its own sake and not for a particular result which the therapist desires. Housing accommodation is provided to deal with housing needs and not for personal pathology, and money is provided for financial needs. Recreation and education have their own justification for the development of individuals at every stage of life. Even within a medical framework there are treatments which aim more at developing the normal capacity than at curing disease. When activities are directed to pathology, to performance, to the interaction, or to some necessary provision, the benefits in the first place should be judged by the satisfaction of the primary aim. Any other benefit is a bonus.

There may be arguments as to what constitutes therapy. We have attempted to define the target of treatment within the different frames of reference which we have disucssed. Within the medical model, which, for all the attacks made upon it, survives and gives service to a whole range of disorders (specific entities of disease), the target is the pathology. We have extended the dimensions of diagnosis to include dysfunctions and deviations. The targets in one case may be some

normal functions; in the other the aim is either conformity or tolerance
of the deviation.

Emerging from the diagnostic framework, we may direct treatment
to the interaction, the maturational process, or to some particular one
of the primary processes of provision. Here it may well be that what we
offer as treatment is some very ordinary component of ordinary life
which has hitherto been neglected. This will be beneficial, but it is
misleading to give the name of "therapy" to this treatment if we are
implying that the treatment is being directed to the pathology
indicative of an identifiable disorder. The task remains, however, to
define one's aim even when it ceases to be based on the concept of
disorder which has to be identified with the question, "What is it, what
caused it, and how do we treat it?"

We need to try to recognize the nature of the good work we do with a
personal part of our personalities.

Professional practice which is based upon exact knowledge is
constantly increasing along with advances in the knowledge which is
employed. This forms a large part of the work of any profession. At the
same time the area of uncertainty grows at an even faster rate along with
the demand to deal with what is unsatisfactory. Something must remain
outside the range of existing knowledge because the standards by which
satisfaction are judged are essentially indefinable. It seems to be the fate
of some branches of the professions of medicine, of education, and of
social work to linger in the areas of uncertainty. They may envy those
who are able to confine themselves to definable tasks, where cause and
effect are clearly related. These are the areas of certainty. The existence
of reliable knowledge is a protection to the personality of the worker,
even when the processes are difficult.

The work which is on the fringe of knowledge involves the worker's
personality in his activities. He carries the burden of making a choice
between exact opposites: the alternatives of holding and withholding,
the engagement of his own love and hate with the loves and hates of
those with whom he works. He is unable to set limits to the aspects of
personality that are the subject of his work when dealing with mental
disorder. He is, at the same time, dealing with every aspect of normal
feelings and relationships. By going beyond the psychiatric syndromes
he come to realize that every one is more sane and more insane than at

first appearance. The insane all have areas of sanity and they also may have unplumbed depths of psychosis which are not yet comprehended. What, therefore, do we try to understand? The sane part? Or the insane part? How big or small a fraction of a personality do we need to make contact with? The illusion of a whole personality is only maintained by finding ways of ignoring the part that we do not understand. Even with the insane, we may find enough normality to be able to attempt to satisfy some common human needs. It does not make the person sane, but it is possible to work with the sane part. With wider knowledge about the insane part it becomes possible to separate the syndromes and to use that knowledge as a basis of treatment which is directed to the psychotic process itself.

The description of the psychiatric syndromes represents observations from the past which must be respected, conserved, and transferred to other professions. They represent all that we have in the way of certainty about mental disorder. We have to sacrifice the certainty when dealing with mental activities that transcend the syndromes. Certainty seemed to be easier to maintain when it was customary to draw a sharp boundary line between sanity and insanity.

The Good-enough Worker

The area of uncertainty is also an area of creativity which is shared by the arts and sciences. It involves the same human functions which constitute the relationships between human beings, particularly the relationship between parents and children. Winnicott used the phrase the "good-enough mother" and this could be transferred to the idea of a "good-enough professional worker". It is quite sufficient to be good enough in those situations where all that one can do is to stand by and use the opportunity to apply any available skills and resources which may produce a small gain. The self-doubts can yield to some degree of satisfaction with the recognition that one is sharing a universal human experience.

As always, Shakespeare has illuminated this limit to the capacity to demand success. It has been conjectured that his plays are his attempts to portray human personality in all its variants: the sonnets give a clue to the personality of Shakespeare himself. His own position as an actor

and a playwright must at times have compared disadvantageously with
the apparently settled lives of some members of the nobility with whom
he had intimate contact. Sonnet No. 29 reveals a despair which he must
frequently have felt. In sonnet No. 30 there are indications of
depression, but the last two lines carry him back, somewhat abruptly,
to his normality. In sonnet No. 29, the counter-balancing thoughts, in
which he finds external support, come earlier and more gradually.

> When, in disgrace with fortune and men's eyes,
> I all alone beweep my outcast state,
> And trouble deaf heaven with my bootless cries,
> And look upon myself, and curse my fate,
> Wishing me like to one more rich in hope,
> Featured like him, like him with friends possess'd,
> Desiring this man's art and that man's scope,
> With what I most enjoy contented least;
> Yet in these thoughts myself most despising,
> Haply I think on thee, and then my state,
> Like to the lark at break of day arising,
> From sullen earth, sings hymns at heaven's gate;
> For thy sweet love remember'd such wealth brings
> That then I scorn to change my state with kings.

Similar thoughts will preoccupy any person who uses for his work
the same processes that more fortunate people can reserve for their
personal lives. Where the subject of work involves the common
expression of living and loving, of growing up and growing old, of
separations and of unions, and of elation and despair, it may be
impossible for the worker to put himself at a professional distance.
Moreover, he may not be able to distinguish between the contribution
which comes from the trained part of his personality and that which
comes from the untrained personal self. It is the engagement of that
personal part of the self which puts the worker at risk.

It follows, therefore, that when the worker has no other assignment
than to offer care and support, it is the precise moment when he himself
is in most need of that care and support himself. He is asked to give
care and support in those stages of his career before he has acquired
technical experience. He is called upon, once again, to give care and
support when, at the height of his skill, he is venturing into areas
beyond those in which his hard-won skills are applicable. At both these
stages the writings which record established theory and practice are

insufficient. Professions need in the first place the authority which comes from the possession of a theoretical body of knowledge. Professions, moreover, are recognized by the competence with which tasks are carried out and by the observance of a discipline which ensures that the work is undertaken for the benefit of the patient. When, however, the task carries the worker's own personality into the engagement, and when he is called upon to go beyond the range of established experience, the worker has to turn for support to the writings of poets and priests who have been able to enter the lower depths and find value in what they discovered there. It is this communion with those who have, throughout the ages, found the language to express human despair and aspirations that confirms the "good-enough" worker in an occupation that he would scorn to change.

Those who can respond to the cry for help from others are those who have been able to recognize, and find help, for their own needs.

Further Reading

ASHER, RICHARD (Ed. Sir Francis Avery Jones), *Talking Sense*, Pitman Medical (1972).

BALINT, M., *The Basic Fault*, Tavistock Publications (1968).

CLARE, ANTHONY, *Psychiatry in Dissent*, Tavistock Publications (1976).

COOK, NORMAN D., *Stability and Flexibility*, Pergamon Press (Systems, Science and World Order Library) (1980).

DAWS, D. AND BOSTON, M., *The Child Psychotherapist* (2nd ed.), Wildwood House (1981).

FREUD, ANNA, *Normality and Pathology in Childhood*, Hogarth Press (1966).

GREENSON, RALPH R. *The Technique and Practice of Psychoanalysis* (Vol. 1), Hogarth Press (1967).

HALEY, JAY, *Problem Solving Therapy*, Jossey Bass (1976).

KAHN, J.H., *Job's Illness*, Pergamon Press (1975).

KAHN, J.H. AND WRIGHT, S.E., *Human Growth and Development of Personality* (3rd ed.), Pergamon Press (1980).

KAHN, J.H., NURSTEN, J.P., AND CARROLL, H.C.M., *Unwillingly to School* (3rd ed.), Pergamon Press (1981).

MAHLER, MARGARET, PINE, FRED, and BERGMAN, ANNI, *The Psychological Birth of the Human Infant*, Hutchinson (1975).

PINCUS, LILY, *Death and the Family*, Pantheon Books (1974).

PINCUS, LILY and DARE, CHRISTOPHER *Secrets in the Family*, Faber & Faber (1978).

ROBINSON, DAVID, *The Process of Becoming Ill*, Routledge & Kegan Paul (1971).

RUTTER, M., MAUGHAN, B., MORTIMORE, P., and OUSTON, J., *Fifteen Thousand Hours: Secondary Schools and Their Effects on Children*, Open Books (1975).

SKYNNER, A. C. ROBIN, *One Flesh, Separate Persons*, Constable (1976).

STORR, ANTHONY, *The Art of Psychotherapy*, Heinemann (1979).

THOMPSON, S. and KAHN, J.H., *The Group Process as a Helping Technique*, Pergamon Press (1970).

TUCKETT, DAVID, *Introduction to Medical Sociology*, Tavistock Publications (1976).

WINNICOTT, D.W., *The Family and Individual Development*, Tavistock Publications (1965).

General Reading

DONNE, JOHN, "Death's Duell": his last sermon delivered at the beginning of Lent, 1630.
ELIOT, GEORGE, *Middlemarch*.
HILL, SUSAN, *The Albatross*, Penguin Books (1970).
HOBAN, RUSSELL, *Kleinzeit*, Picador (Pan Books) (1976).

Index

131